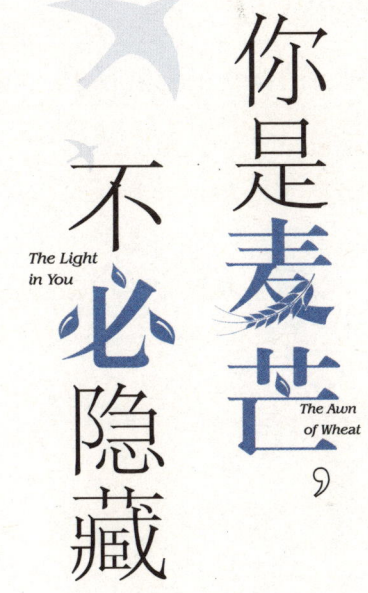

你是麦芒，不必隐藏

The Light in You

The Awn of Wheat

《意林·绘英语》编辑部 —— 编

吉林摄影出版社
·长春·

图书在版编目（CIP）数据

你是麦芒，不必隐藏：汉、英 /《意林·绘英语》
编辑部编. -- 长春：吉林摄影出版社，2018.8
（彩绘英文）
ISBN 978-7-5498-3705-2

Ⅰ.①你… Ⅱ.①意… Ⅲ.①故事—作品集—世界—汉、英 Ⅳ.①I14

中国版本图书馆CIP数据核字(2018)第176493号

你是麦芒，不必隐藏　NI SHI MAIMANG, BUBI YINCANG

项目出品	松果阅读
出 版 人	孙洪军
主　　编	顾 平　杜普洲
责任编辑	施 岚　孙 瑜
总 策 划	蔡 燕
丛书统筹	赵添天
策划编辑	赵添天　陈佳怡
执行编辑	纪宛伯　陈佳怡
设计总监	资 源
封面设计	徐 丹
美术编辑	陈 星
开　　本	16.6mm×24mm　1/16
字　　数	200千字
印　　张	12
版　　次	2018年8月第1版
印　　次	2018年8月第1次印刷
出　　版	吉林摄影出版社
发　　行	吉林摄影出版社
地　　址	长春市泰来街1825号
	邮　编：130062
电　　话	总编办：0431-86012616
	发行科：0431-86012602
网　　址	www.jlsycbs.net
经　　销	全国各地新华书店
印　　刷	小森印刷（北京）有限公司
书　　号	ISBN 978-7-5498-3705-2　　　定　价：36.90元

启　事

本书编选时参阅了部分报刊和著作，我们未能与部分作品的文字作者、漫画作者以及插画作者取得联系，在此深表歉意。请各位作者见到本书后及时与我们联系，以便按国家相关规定支付稿酬及赠送样书。

地址：北京市朝阳区南磨房路37号华腾北搪商务大厦1501室《意林》编辑部（100022）
电话：010-51900482

版权所有　翻印必究
（如发现印装质量问题，请与承印厂联系退换）

目录 Contents

第一章: *Girl Power* 女孩力量

002 I'm Going to Keep Going until I succeed—or Die
在我成功或死去之前，我不会停下脚步 / 译◎朱　莉

004 Nobody Knows What the Future Will Be, That's Why We Rebel and Do Crazy Things
没人知道未来怎样，所以需要叛逆和疯狂 / 演唱◎艾玛·斯通

008 I Don't Want to Go to School
我不想上学 / 译◎朱　莉

012 Mistakes Don't Make Damaged, They Make You Clean
错误不会毁掉你，而是让你透彻清净 / 文◎佚　名

018 Girl, You Should Spend More Time Being
女孩，你要用更多时间存在 / 文◎斯堪特里·斯帕

020 Clean
清净 / 演唱◎泰勒·斯威夫特

024 It's Not Necessary for Every Girl to Be Ivanka
不是每个女孩都要成为伊万卡 / 文◎斯堪特里·斯帕

027 Destiny
命运 / 文◎佚　名

029 Staying Up all Night is not Motivational 熬夜不是励志/文◎佚　名

030 But don't Worry,You Will Someday 总有一天，你会明白/文◎佚　名

031 Life is a series of Waiting 人生是一连串的等待/文◎佚　名

032 Burn 全力燃烧/文◎杰克·凯鲁亚克

033 No Doubt about My Dream
对梦想从未有过疑虑 / 文◎窦靖童

036 Gap Year or Not? The Biggest Risk in Life Is Not Taking One at All
该不该选择间隔年？人生最大的冒险是不去冒险/文◎佚　名

042 *Proofreader Girl Kono Etsuko: A Boring Job Is So Great*
《校对女孩河野悦子》：无趣的工作，万岁 / 文◎小　J

044 *Seventeen*
17 岁 / 文◎椎名林檎

047 *J.K. Rowing Is My Hero*
J.K. 罗琳是我的英雄 / 文◎蕾切尔

054 *Emma Watson: You Can Be a Warrior*
艾玛·沃特森：你可以成为战士 / 译◎阿　诺

058 *Chen Man: Changing How the World Sees China*
陈漫：改变外国人看待中国的方式 / 译◎阿　诺

062 *Lady Gaga Talks about the Downsides of Fame*
出名真的好吗？Lady Gaga 告诉你 / 译◎亚　琪

066 *Take Your Broken Heart, Make It into Art*
带着你的破碎之心，去创造艺术吧 / 文◎梅丽尔·斯特里普

071 *What Did You Done to the Girls When You Ask Them to Be Pretty, Small, and Quiet*
当你要求女生娇小可人又文静的时候，她们遭受了什么 / 文◎丽莎·卡普雷托

074 *Wu Yishu Wins Chinese Ancient Poetry Competition and Lots of Fans*
武亦姝夺冠《中国诗词大会》，圈粉无数 / 文◎陶祥飞

078 *A Girl Between Two Worlds*
行走在两个世界的女孩 / 文◎曼迪·卢

083 *If You've Got a Dollar, There's Plenty to Share*
你只要有一美元，就有很多东西可以分享 / 文◎蕾哈娜

086 *Dreamlike Childhood*
梦 / 文◎冰　心

090 *Emma Watson: The Most Beautiful Girls Are Those Who Have Strong Heart*
艾玛·沃特森：内心强大的女性最美丽 / 文◎艾玛·沃特森

095 *Be Proud of Who You Are*
为自己骄傲 / 文◎凯特·佩里

098 *A Girl*
少女 / 文◎庞　德

第二章: *Madman's Diary* 狂人日记

100　*The Value of Time*
　　时间的价值/文◎凯瑟琳·桑

102　*As Heroine of Every Mundane Day*
　　平凡日子里的女英雄/译◎朱　莉

104　*Quotes of First Ladies: I Don't Want to Be a Saddle Horse*
　　我不愿成为一匹驯马——那些美国第一夫人的名言/文◎佚　名

107　*Think Different*
　　非同凡响/文◎佚　名

第三章: *YOLO* 只活一次

110　*Motto of Youth: YOLO*
　　当下年轻人的座右铭——YOLO/文◎亚　宁

111　*I Am Not Pretty. I Am Not Beautiful. I Am as Radiant as the Sun*
　　我不可爱，我也不漂亮，但我也能和太阳一样耀眼/文◎佚　名

112　*It's Okay to Be Different*
　　不一样没关系/文◎托德·帕尔

116　*It Is a Lot More Dangerous for a Plane to Stay on the Ground*
　　待在地上的飞机更危险/文◎佚　名

118　*You are One of a Kind*
　　独一无二的你/文◎佚　名

121　*10 Things to Do Even if They Judge You*
　　即使别人评头论足，也要去做的10件事/文◎马　克

130　*You Should Become a Conduit of Light*
　　你要成为自己的那道光/文◎艾米丽·马歇尔

132　*Are You That Elephant Stuck Right Where You Were*
　　你也是那头被困住的大象吗/文◎佚　名

134　*Circle*
　　圈/文◎张智中

136　*Don't Be What They Make You*
　　别按"他们"的期待过你自己的人生/文◎休·杰克曼

138　You Have to Be You, Before You Can Be Them
　　　在成为他们之前，请先成为你自己 / 译◎朱　莉

142　Each One of Us Is Alone in the World
　　　我们生来就是孤独的——《月亮与六便士》/ 文◎毛　姆

144　The Life I Desired
　　　我所追求的生活 / 文◎毛　姆

147　Moonlight: At Some Point, You Gotta Decide for Yourself Who You're Going to Be
　　　《月光男孩》：总有一天，你要自己决定成为什么样的人 / 文◎佚　名

第四章：*Freckle Girl*　雀斑少女

150　How the First Ladies Take the Fashion Lead
　　　历任美国第一夫人是如何引领时尚潮流的 / 文◎莎拉·杨

155　Homely Looking People Will Not Easily Go Die
　　　没有颜值的人不会轻易投降 / 文◎佚　名

159　Is It True that Imperfection Is the real Fashion? Western Girls Are Crazy about Freckles Tattoos
　　　原来不完美才是真流行？欧美少女都在迷雀斑刺青 / 文◎佚　名

162　Here's to the Girls Who Don't Wear Makeup
　　　献给那些不化妆的女孩 / 文◎佚　名

164　You Can Set the Standards on Beauty by Yourself
　　　无须别人告诉你什么才是美丽 / 文◎佚　名

166　How Can You Be the New It Girl
　　　如何成为一个崭新的酷女孩 / 文◎佚　名

171　Learn to Love the Person in the Mirror
　　　试着爱镜中的自己 / 文◎佚　名

177　I Was Wearing a Wig, No One Could Be Perfect Like that
　　　我戴的是假发，没有人能长那么完美 / 文◎艾米莉亚·克拉克

179　I Was Embarrassed about My Ear
　　　我的耳朵曾经让我很尴尬 / 文◎佚　名

181　Let's Learn How to Keep Smile
　　　想当社交达人？先学会保持微笑吧 / 文◎佚　名

第一章

Girl Power
女孩力量

I'm Going to Keep Going until I Succeed — or Die

文◎ anonymous

One of the interesting things about Los Angeles is that most of the people living in the city are here for a common goal: to work in the entertainment industry. Not all of the people who come here to try this are going to make it, or at least not at the level that they want to or dream about. That can be a bit soul crushing. It really is a magical moment when things work out. But there is no one size fits all recipe on how to "make it" in this industry. How to deal with the moments when you thought about quitting, listen to how Emma Stone says.

Ahead of the Academy Awards on this year, Stone — who is nominated for her leading role in best picture nominee *La La Land*— passed on her wisdom to fellow dreamers in Hollywood.

"That's a big question," said Stone, 28, about her advice to those who are pursuing their dreams in the entertainment industry. "I think it's a very individual question."

The actress added: "Just keep going. Through any situation… If you're going through hell, keep going."

In *La La Land*, Stone plays an aspiring actress living in Hollywood who is pursuing her dream of making it in front of the camera. Towards the end of the film, Stone performs

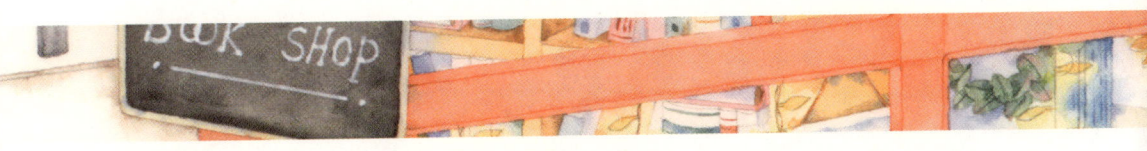

an "Audition" song, which has inspiring lyrics for those in pursuit of their dreams: "Here's to the ones who dream / Foolish as they may seem / Here's to the hearts that ache / Here's to the mess we make."

在我成功或死去之前，我不会停下脚步

译◎ Julie（朱莉）

洛杉矶最有意思的一点是，大多数住在这儿的人都有同一个目标：进娱乐圈工作。但并不是所有来这儿的人都能实现梦想，或者说达到他们想要的那个高度。这是挺打击人的。梦想实现的时刻如魔术般美妙。但在这个圈子里，没有一劳永逸的通吃法则。如何面对那些想放弃的时刻呢？听听艾玛·斯通怎么说。

在 2017 年的奥斯卡颁奖典礼之前，作为奥斯卡最佳影片奖提名《爱乐之城》的女主角，艾玛·斯通向好莱坞的其他追梦者们传授了自己的经验。

"这是一个很大的问题，"谈到对在娱乐圈打拼的人的建议，28 岁的艾玛·斯通说，"我认为这个问题因人而异。"

她接着说："无论你处在什么样的困境中，都要不断前行。即使你在地狱中也要坚持下去。"

在《爱乐之城》中，斯通饰演一个住在好莱坞有理想有抱负的女演员，她一直坚持着自己的演员梦。在电影的结尾，艾玛·斯通演唱了一首叫《试镜》的歌曲，歌词对追梦者有振奋人心的力量："为追梦者歌唱 / 他们看似愚笨 / 唱给我们疼痛的心 / 唱给曾经犯下的错。"

洛杉矶有成千上万和米娅一样栖身于这座梦幻之城并且等待机会的人。他们需要忍耐一次又一次的忽视和拒绝，任由自尊和热忱被消磨殆尽。在一次又一次失败之后，终于被伯乐发现的米娅，在试镜时即兴表演了歌曲《痴梦人》，她唱出了自己，也让无数追求梦想的人落泪。致那些心怀梦想的傻子，尽管在别人看来愚蠢透顶；致那些没有人知道的未来，所以人生需要叛逆和疯狂。

Nobody Knows What the Future Will Be, That's Why We Rebel and Do Crazy Things

singer ◎ Emma · Stone

My aunt used to live in Paris
I remember she used to come home and tell us
These stories about being abroad and

I remember she told that us she jumped in the river once

Barefoot

She smiled

Leapt without looking

And tumbled into the Seine

The water was freezing

She spent a month sneezing

But said she would do it again

Here's to the ones

Who dream

Foolish as they may seem

Here's to the hearts

That ache

Here's to the mess

We make

She captured a feeling

Sky with no ceiling

The sunset inside a frame

She lived in her liquor

And died with a flicker

I'll always remember the flame

Here's to the ones

Who dream

Foolish as they may seem

Here's to the hearts

That ache

Here's to the mess

We make

She told me

A bit of madness is key

To give us new colors to see

Who knows where it will lead us

And that's why they need us

So bring on the rebels
The ripples from pebbles
The painters and poets and plays
And here's to the fools
Who dream
Crazy as they may seem
Here's to the hearts that break
Here's to the mess we make
I trace it all back
To then
Her and the snow and the Seine
Smiling through it
She said
She'd do it again

没人知道未来怎样，所以需要叛逆和疯狂

演唱◎ Emma Stone（艾玛·斯通）

我的姑姑曾经住在巴黎
我记得，她总给我们讲在国外生活的点点滴滴
跳河的一次经历
脱掉鞋子
她微笑着
然后闭上双眼，纵身跃下
跌入塞纳河中
冰冷刺骨的河水

让她打了一个月的喷嚏

但她说，若能重来她仍会再一次跳下

向那些怀揣梦想的人致敬

哪怕在旁人眼里，他们愚蠢而自命不凡

向那些受尽讥讽的梦想致敬

向那些我们犯下的错误致敬

她捕捉到了那种感觉

或许是在无垠的深空之外

或是被嵌在画框里的晚霞之中

她是用烈酒酿成的仙女

如蜡炬上的火苗一般狂舞直至成为灰烬

她的炽热与光芒，我永远不会遗忘

向那些怀揣梦想的人致敬

哪怕在旁人眼里，他们愚蠢而自命不凡

向那些受尽讥讽的梦想致敬

向那些我们犯下的错误致敬

她曾告诉我

不疯癫

不成活

谁知道人类将走向何方

而这就是我们存在的意义

那么来打碎腐朽陈旧吧，来冲破循规蹈矩吧

连卵石丢入水中都能激起层层涟漪

更何况绘画、诗集和一幕幕戏剧

向那些理想主义的傻瓜致敬

哪怕在旁人眼里，他们偏执而狂妄自大

向那些被现实压碎的梦想致敬

向那些我们曾犯下的错误致敬

当我如今回眸

她，站在雪地上，站在塞纳河边

微笑着，岿然不动

她说，一切若能重来

我心依旧如故

At school I didn't expect everyone to like me and they certainly didn't.
在学校我从不指望每个人都喜欢我，显然那是不可能的。
——Alex Chung（艾里珊·钟）

I Don't Want to Go to School

文© anonymous

These are top 10 reasons why students don't go to school.

1. Homework.
2. Bullying.
3. Lack of respect.
4. Boring.
5. The endless drone of the fact that you are no good and never will be.
6. Not a social extrovert butterfly.
7. No good at sports.
8. Rules.
9. Sitting still for far too long.
10. Lack of expression.

Japanese model Mizuhara Kiko, with her own style and beauty that not everyone would appreciate, used to avoid school. Though she knows how to show her strength in front

of the camera, Mizuhara hasn't always been so confident. Growing up in Kobe, in the Japanese countryside, she often struggled with her mixed-race identity. (Her father is from Texas, and her mother is a Japanese woman of Korean descent.)

"When I went to school, I felt really embarrassed," she recalls. "My dad is American. He looked so different — blond hair, blue eyes, super tall. And I also didn't want anyone to find out that my mom was Korean."

Because of this, Mizuhara avoided speaking English (to the detriment of her fluency) in an effort to fit in.

"I told my dad to stop coming to school. I started wearing the same clothes as other kids. I tried to hide myself — my real self." When she moved to Tokyo at 16 to pursue modeling, she met other mixed-race models and began "opening up."

"I felt stronger. I started to explore my roots, to try to understand my parents," Mizuhara says. "Being original is sometimes difficult in Japan, but there are a lot of original people in Tokyo." Kiko Mizuhara's interest in experiencing other cultures has taken her around the world.

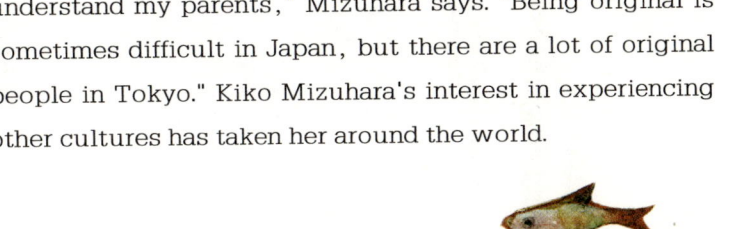

我不想上学

译◎ Julie（朱莉）

学生不想上学有十大原因：

1. 作业。
2. 霸凌。
3. 不被尊重。
4. 无聊。
5. 总有一个喋喋不休的声音在说：你不够好，永远不够。
6. 不是一个爱社交的外向型花蝴蝶。
7. 不擅长体育。
8. 规矩。
9. 要长时间坐着不动。
10. 缺乏表现的机会。

拥有并非人人都能欣赏的独特风格的日本模特水原希子，也有一段不愿上学的时光。如今对于在镜头前秀出自己优势驾轻就熟的她，也不是一直都如此自信。在日本神户乡下长大的水原，曾一度为自己的混血身份挣扎——她的父亲是美国得克萨斯州人，妈妈是有韩国血统的日本女人。

"我上学的时候，真的觉得很尴尬。"她回忆道，"我父亲是美国人，他看起来那么不同——金发碧眼，身高出众。并且我也不想任何人知道我妈妈是韩国人。"

为了合群，水原一直避免说英语（这害得她英文不太流利）。

"我要我爸爸别到学校来。我开始和其他孩子穿一样的衣服。我开始隐藏自己——真实的自己。" 直到16岁，她为了模特事业搬到东京，遇到其他混血模特，才开始"打开"自己。

"我感到自己更有力量了。我开始探索自己的故乡，尝试理解我的父母。"水原说道，"在日本做个怪人有时并不容易，但东京有很多特立独行的人。" 如今，对体验别国文化感兴趣的水原希子已经游览了世界上的很多国家。

> Mistake is what makes people look lovely.
> 错误才是使人显得真正可爱的东西。
> ——Goethe（歌德）

歌德说过，有的人不犯错误，那是因为他从来不去做任何值得做的事。时常处于舆论中心的小天后泰勒·斯威夫特不怕犯错，对于名声带来的过度关注，她的选择是——"做无畏生活中的放大镜"。在1989世界巡回演唱会(The 1989 World Tour)上，泰勒在演唱 *Clean* 之前的一段独白对不自信的人是一剂强心针，"你不是别人眼中定义的那个不完美的自己，你是自己内心定义的美好与价值"。也许这就是偶像的价值，在你还不够强大的时候，让你相信光芒存在于自己的头顶。

Mistakes Don't Make Damaged, They Make You Clean

文◎ anonymous

I think for me, having a magnifying glass on my life has been a good thing and kind of a difficult thing at times, because you feel like you literally just can't get away with anything. Sometimes you're like, wow, if I make a mistake, that's gonna be, that's gonna be everywhere. And because everything that I do, its gonna be documented, and in computers forever. It makes me think about what the little kid in the front row would think, and what my grandchildren would think one day of I made this choice or that choice. I think it's kind of a good governing tool that makes you more responsible for how you act.

You're seeing all these angles of your own life, and

then you compare it to other people's lives. When you don't see what they're going through, you just see the good parts of what they're going through.

When you start to compare yourselves to other people, please change the channel in your mind to something else. Because I think that when it comes to how we see ourselves, other people are really mean, but we're really mean to ourselves. And so it's easy to get confused. And when you do get confused, and you start feeling like you're not special, or you're not different, or you have nothing important to say. We all feel like that sometimes, but what I want you to do right now is, if there's one thing you remember from tonight, remember what I'm about to say.

You need to look into the mirror in the morning, and not tell yourself that you're not special, or you're not good enough, you're not pretty, or you're not awesome.

I'm gonna tell you right now the things you actually are not. These are the things you really are not.

You are not the opinion of somebody who doesn't know you.

You are not damaged goods just because you made mistakes in your life.

You are not going nowhere just because you haven't gotten where you want to go yet. Those are the things you actually are not.

Now, I want to tell you what you are.

You are your own definition of beautiful and worthwhile, that's what you are.

You are someone who is wiser because you made

mistakes, not damaged, wiser.

You are somebody who could be at this moment, right now, sitting there, there, there.

You are going through whatever you're going through in your life, that's stressing you out, or confusing you ,or making you upset.

But you got out of bed and put on an awesome outfit, and you came to a concert, and now we're all having the best time ever on a Wednesday night.

You know it's not about perfection, it's about just getting on with things sometimes. You have just to get credit for getting up and going on with things.

You don't have to do it perfectly.

And I think that we mistake our mistakes for damage and we think other people were judge us for them. But I want you to know the way that I see mistakes. They don't make damaged, they make you clean.

错误不会毁掉你，而是让你透彻清净

文◎佚名

我认为对我来说，生活中有一个放大镜算是一件好事，当然有时候也会比较艰难，因为你会感觉到你犯一点点错误都会被逮住。有时候好像你犯了一个错误，所有人都会知道。因为我做的每一件事都会被记录下来，都会永远留在电脑里。我就想知道，自己做出决定的时候，坐在前排的小孩儿会怎么想，我的孙辈会怎么想。我觉得这也算是一个很好的自我管理工具，让你对自己的行为更加负责。

你看到自己人生中的种种事情，然后拿来和别人的生活做对比。但你并不知道他们真实的经历，只是看到他们生活中光鲜的一面。

当你拿自己和别人做对比的时候，我希望你能把心思放在其他事情上。因为我觉得当我们审视自我的时候，别人的观点是很严苛的，而我们对自己也一样非常刻薄尖锐。两相冲突就会令人困扰。当你倍感困惑的时候，当你觉得自己流于平庸，平凡无奇，甚至觉得自己不值一提。人人都会有类似的感受，但我现在希望，如果今夜有什么能刻在你脑海中，我希望你记住我下面说的话。

你每天早晨起床，看着镜子里的自己时别说自己平凡无奇，

也别说自己不够好，自己不够漂亮，自己一点儿都不酷。

我现在告诉你，你不是这样子的。这真的不是你。

不了解你的人，他们说的根本不是真实的你。

你犯下的错，并不会毁掉你。

尚无目标，并不意味着你的未来渺茫。这都不是真实的你。

现在我要告诉你，你是怎样的人。

是你自己定义了你的美丽和价值，这才是你。

你是因犯错而愈加理智的人，而不是被毁掉的人，是更加理智。

你生活在当下，就现在，坐在台下这边，那边，还有那边的。

你历经生活中的种种，就算它们令你倍感压力，令你困惑，或者令你沮丧。

但你清早起床，好好打扮，来看这演唱会，又能和我们一起享受这最美好的周三夜晚。

你知道,这无关完美,而是在某些时候去大方应对,有时你还会因积极应对而获得称赞。

你没有必要事事完美。

我觉得我们误以为错误会毁掉自己,我们生怕别人借此评头论足。但我想让你知道,我是如何看待过错的。错误不会毁掉你,而是会让你透彻清净。

Girl, You Should Spend More Time Being

文◎ Sanctuary Spa

If I were young woman now I'm not sure I want to cope.

With all the things you have; the opportunities, the technology. I'd like to think it could be a world of pleasure. But I fear instead it would only be a world of pressure.

If I had my time again, I wouldn't create a "to do" list, I'd created "to don't do" list.

What I wouldn't give to extend those goodnight kisses instead of moaning about having to get up early in the

morning.

What I wouldn't give for 5 more minutes on the dance floor while my legs were still strong enough to carry me.

There's the most important word, being.

Being lost in the moment.

Being at peace with the world.

Believe me, if I were a young woman now, I'd spend more time being, not doing.

女孩,你要用更多时间存在

文◎ Sanctuary Spa(斯堪特里·斯帕)

如果我现在是一个年轻的女孩子,我大概不知该如何应对。

看看你们现在拥有的那些东西,那些机遇和高科技。我会想,这大概是一个快乐的世界吧。但是我担心,相反地,这只是一个充满压力的世界。

如果我能回到过去,我不会列一个"要做的事情"清单,我会列一个"不要做的事情"清单。

我愿不惜一切换来更漫长的午夜吻别,而不是抱怨着明天要早起。

我会不惜一切在舞池中多待 5 分钟,那时我的双脚还能强有力地站立。

最重要的那个词就是:存在。

存在,并沉浸于那一刻。

存在,并与世界和平相处。

相信我,如果我现在是一个年轻的女孩子,我会用更多的时间去"存在",而不是"做"。绘英语

Clean

Singer ◎ Taylor Swift

The drought was the very worst

When the flowers that we'd grown together died of thirst

It was months and months of back and forth

You're still all over me like a wine stained dress I can't wear anymore

Hung my head as I lost the war

And sky turned to black like a perfect storm

Rain came pouring down when I was drowning

That's when I could finally breathe

By morning gone was any trace of you

I think I am finally clean

There was nothing left to do

When the butterflies turned to dust that covered my whole room

So I punched a hole in the roof

I let the flood carry away all my pictures of you

The water filled my lungs

I screamed so loud but no one heard a thing

Rain came pouring down when I was drowning

That's when I could finally breathe

And by morning, gone was any trace of you

I think I am finally clean

I think I am finally clean

Said I think I am finally clean

10 months sober

I must admit

Just because you're clean don't mean you don't miss it

10 months older

I won't give in

Now that I'm clean I'm never gonna risk it

The drought was the very worst

When the flowers that we'd grown together died of thirst

Rain came pouring down when I was drowning

That's when I could finally breathe

And by morning, gone was any trace of you

I think I am finally clean

Finally clean

Think I am finally clean

Think I am finally clean

清净

演唱◎ Taylor Swift（泰勒·斯威夫特）

这里贫瘠如同荒漠

当我们一起种的花因饥渴而凋零

这场长达数月的来回拉锯

而你仍让我没辙，如同沾有酒渍的连衣裙，我再也无法穿着

我已经被你羞辱得低下了头，仿佛这场战争我已败北

天空被黑暗入侵，像无懈可击的风暴

雨倾盆而下，我慢慢沉溺

但此时我才终于能呼吸
而那个早晨你无法寻觅
我想我终于清净,不再留恋
已经无事可做
蝴蝶化为灰烬飘落整个房间
所以我在屋顶开了一个洞
让洪水带走你所有的照片
水浸满我的肺
我大声尖叫却无人听见
雨倾盆而下,我慢慢沉溺
但此时我才终于能呼吸
而那个早晨你无法寻觅
我想我终于清净,不再留恋
我想我终于清净,不再留恋
看吧,我想我终于彻底放下
十个月的冷静
我无法否认
只因你说你已释怀并不意味着你不再留恋
十个月的成长
我不会屈服
既然我已释怀我就绝不会再次冒险
这里贫瘠如同荒漠
当我们一起种的花因饥渴凋零
雨倾盆而下,我慢慢沉溺
但此时我才终于能呼吸
而那个早晨你无法寻觅
我想我终于释怀
不再留恋
我想我终于释怀
不再留恋

It's Not Necessary for Every Girl to Be Ivanka

文◎ Sanctuary Spa

Ever since Donald Trump was elected the president of the US, the entire Trump family has been put under a microscope.

In China, the spotlight has been mainly focused on Trump and his daughter Ivanka. She is described on WeChat as an extremely influential role model with stunning beauty, a successful career, and a happy family.

She leads a dream life that a million girls would kill for. Yes, she was born with a silver spoon in her mouth. But she got where she is by her own offorts efforts.

There's always going to be articles that say people born into wealthy families are better looking and have a better family background than you, but these people do work harder than you.

Are you a loser if you were raised in an ordinary family? Should you feel guilty that you sleep eight hours a day because Ivanka sleeps five?

If you just want to keep a stable nine-to-five job, does it mean you are not ambitious?

How about if you don't work out or eat healthy, does that mean you will not find your Mr or Miss Right?

There is a tendency in media nowadays to encourage elitism.

They are trying to brainwash young people into thinking that they should invest an enormous amount of time and money in bodybuilding and appearance enhancement, even plastic surgery.

They encourage lifestyle makeovers: wine tasting classes and expensive trips overseas.

They make you believe that if you do as they say, you can improve the quality of your life and join the elites.

But what's the downside of being mediocre? Do you really need to go to the gym five days a week unless you are a gym maniac?

Do you need to take hundreds of selfies and Photoshop the selected ones to post on WeChat?

Do you really need to break your neck and sacrifice to earn your first pot of gold only to worry constantly about how to blend into high society later?

Don't let the idea of elitism get to you. Everybody has a right to the life they want.

Human beings should not be judged as a success or failure based on whether they are a part of the elite or not.

As long as you lead a happy and comfortable life, why bother to chase after other people's shadows? Choose your own life path and go for it.

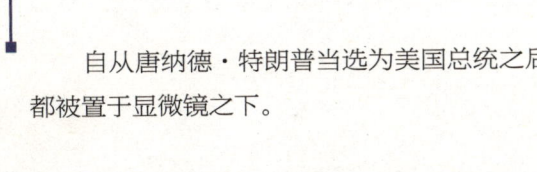

不是每个女孩都要成为伊万卡

文◎ Sanctuary Spa（斯堪特里·斯帕）

自从唐纳德·特朗普当选为美国总统之后，整个特朗普家族都被置于显微镜之下。

在中国，人们主要关注特朗普和他的女儿伊万卡。人们在微信上将伊万卡描述为一个具有耀眼美貌而又影响力非凡的人物，她有成功的事业和一个快乐的家庭。

她过着上百万女孩极度渴望的梦幻般的生活。是的，她是含着银汤匙出生的。但是她是靠自己的努力才取得现在的成就的。

总是有一些文章说那些出生在富贵之家的人要长得比你好看、有更好家庭背景，但是这些人工作也要比你更加努力一些。

如果在一个平民之家长大，你就注定是一个失败者吗？因为伊万卡一天只睡5小时，所以你就该为自己睡了8小时而感到内疚吗？

如果你只想维持一份稳定的朝九晚五的工作，那就意味着你没有抱负吗？

如果你不健身或者饮食不健康，那就意味着你不可能找到自己的真命天子/女吗？

现在的媒体都有一种鼓吹精英主义的倾向。

它们试图说服年轻人认为自己应该投入大量的时间和金钱来拥有漂亮的身材和好看的外貌，甚至是整形手术。

它们鼓励生活方式的改变：品酒课和昂贵的海外旅行。

它们使你相信，如果你按照它们说的那样做，你就可以改善自己的生活质量、成为精英。

但是平庸有什么坏处呢？除非你是一个健身狂魔，否则你真的有必要一周去5天健身房吗？

你有必要拍几百张自拍，然后挑选一些修图过后发到微信上去吗？

你真的有必要挤破脑袋、牺牲赚取第一桶金的时机，只为时常担心以后如何融入上流社会吗？

不要成为精英主义思想的俘虏。每个人都有过自己想要的生活的权利。

人类成功或失败，不应该由他是否是一名精英来评判。

只要你过着快乐而舒适的生活，为什么要徒添烦恼去追逐别人的影子呢？选择你自己的道路并坚持走下去吧！绘英语

Destiny

文◎佚名

Everywhere man blames nature and fate,

There's no escaping your destiny.

Yet his fate is mostly but the echo of

his character and passions,

his mistakes and weaknesses.

命运

文◎佚名

我们总是抱怨环境和命运,觉得一切都是天意。

但是,命运其实大部分,

是我们的性格、激情、错误和脆弱使然。 绘英语

Staying Up all Night is not Motivational
熬夜不是励志

文◎佚名

Staying up all night is not motivational, but it is an overdraft in your health. Everyone has reason to be more scared of disease and death than before. Only when you have health can you embrace everything you are eager for and not prematurely say goodbye to anything you have deep affection for. Don't stay up late, sleep early!

熬夜不是励志，而是透支，我们每个人都有理由比以前更害怕疾病和死亡。拥有健康，才能拥抱渴望的一切，才能不过早地跟热爱的一切告别。别熬夜了，早点儿睡吧。绘英语

But don't Worry, You Will Someday
总有一天，你会明白

文◎佚名

I had always heard your entire life flashes in front of your eyes the secondbefore you die. First of all, that one second isn't a second at all. It stretches on forever, like an ocean of time.

For me, it was lying on my back at Boy Scout Camp, watching falling stars. And yellow leaves from the maple trees that lined our street. Or my grandmother's hands, and the way her skin seemed like paper. And the first time I saw my cousin Tony's brand-new Firebird. And Janie, and Janie. And Carolyn.

听说人在死前的一秒钟，他的一生会闪过眼前。首先，其实不是一秒钟，而是延伸成无止境的时间，就像时间的海洋。

对我来说，我的一生是躺在草地上看着流星雨，还有街道上枯黄的枫叶，或是奶奶手上纸一样的皮肤，还有我第一次看到托尼表哥那辆全新的火鸟跑车，还有珍妮，还有卡洛琳。

Life is a series of Waiting
人生是一连串的等待

文◎佚名

Youth and childishness can both bring about the same weakness: lack of patience. Whatever things you do, you want to see the results immediately. Life is a series of waiting. People often start to learn this kind of lesson when they are in the middle age.

年轻和幼稚都会造成同样的弱点：缺乏耐性。无论做什么事，都想马上看到结果。人生就是一连串的等待，这样的教训往往得活到中年才能体会。绘英语

Burn
全力燃烧

文◎杰克·凯鲁亚克

The only people for me are the mad ones, the ones who are mad to live, mad to talk, mad to be saved, desirous of everything at the same time, the ones who never yawn or say a commonplace thing, but burn, burn, burn like fabulous yellow roman candles exploding like spiders across the stars.

对我来说，真正有意义的是那些疯狂的人。他们疯魔般尽情享受生活，疯魔般高谈阔论，疯魔般等待救赎，同时渴望着世间的一切。他们从来不希冀或言及任何平凡的事物，只是全力燃烧，燃烧，就如同熊熊的罗马巨蜡在星空中四散爆开。绘英语

> If plan A doesn't work, I'll go get another new plan A. I don't settle for plan B.
> 如果最优计划失败了，我就再找一个最优计划。我不会退而求其次。

No Doubt about My Dream

文◎ Dou Jingtong

As a kid at school I saw all my peers worrying about what they wanted to do in their future, what their dreams were, what kind of professions they wanted to go for whey they grow older—it never occurred to me to question that—I've always thought that I am going to do music. For some reason in my head I thought that that was already set.

I'm not annoyed or offended that I'm always introduced in the context of my family, but it's refreshing to be introduced through my music rather than something that's irrelevant to my music.

When I grew older I started to realize that music is really broad. What exactly do I want to do? Do I want to be a musician? Do I want to play an instrument? Do I want to be a producer? Am I more into the music business side of things? That was the only question I had to answer in my teens, which I managed to figure out when I was applying for a school that I went to in Michigan. It's called Interlochen, a performing arts academy.

There were only like a few options that I had. Two options. I was either going to go for the vocal major, which was more leaning toward singing opera, or I had the option of singer-song-write program, which I was familiar with - the requirement was to write three original songs for my application. And that's *what I did, which sparked the whole songwriting thing for me. That's when I began to pin down on what I wanted to do.*

The world is waiting for Dou Jingtong to grow up and expecting how "rebellious" she could be. However, Leah Dou is not a born hater. She said "My parents are so open-minded that I don't have to be rebellious." Instead of being "bad" for "being bad", this girl who started making her own decisions from childhood, knows exactly what she wants. She's not that kind of "bad" girl as expected.

对梦想从未有过疑虑

文◎窦靖童

上学的时候，我那些同伴就很迷茫，想着自己长大以后要做什么，梦想是什么，想着自己长大以后会从事什么样的职业。但是我从来没有过这样的疑虑，我一直都知道自己会做音乐。我的脑袋里冥冥之中已经给自己下定了结论。

我并不反感或是抵触自己的家庭带来的影响。但是，如果你们能通过我的音乐来认识我，而不是因为其他与音乐无关的东西，这会让我感觉很振奋。

长大一些后，我发觉音乐的世界真是太广阔了，我就问自己，最想做的是什么音乐呢？我想当作曲家吗？我想当演奏家吗？我想当制作人吗？我对音乐商务更感兴趣吗？这是我年少时的唯一困惑，在我申请密歇根州因特劳肯艺术学院的时候，我一直在试图搞清楚这个问题。

我曾经冒出过几个想法。两个选择，要么是去学声乐专业，学一些唱剧类的课程，要么就是去学作词作曲，这个我比较熟悉。入学要求是写三首原创歌曲，然后我就这样写了，就像是点了一个火星一样，点燃了我写歌的热情。然后我就明白了，这就是我想做的事，钉死了。

全世界都在等窦靖童长大，全世界都在期待她有多叛逆。可窦靖童并不是天生的愤怒家。她表示"我不需要叛逆，因为我的父母很开明"。比起为了叛逆而叛逆，从小就开始为自己做决定的她更知道自己真正想要的是什么。她不是你们心中那个叛逆女孩。

绘英语

> **Not all those who wander are Lost.**
> 流浪的人未必都迷茫。
>
> ——J.R.R.Tolkien

Gap Year or Not? The Biggest Risk in Life Is Not Taking One at All

文◎anonymous

Obama's elder daughter Malia Obama is a full-fledged cultural icon, whose fashion choices and college visits routinely make headlines. For example, a leaked photo appeared to show Malia wearing a T-shirt with the logo for Brooklyn hip-hop group Pro Era, driving record traffic to co-founder Joey Badass' Wikipedia page. Malia was also spotted on the set of HBO's *Girls*, reportedly as part of an internship for creator Lena Dunham(another It Girl in U.S.).

If your teenager is talking about taking a year away from the classroom between high school and college, you may have Malia Obama to thank for that.

But if they're not yet talking about whether to follow her lead, they should be.

Taking time off between high school and college or sometime during the undergraduate years, as Ms Obama is doing before she attends Harvard, has plenty of appeal for high school graduates who don't know what they want out of college or seek to work, travel or volunteer on the sort of schedule that an academic calendar does not allow.

Parents, however, often worry themselves sick over

such talk.

While no one wants to drop a six-figure sum on a teenager who doesn't want to be in school, there are often nagging doubts over whether students who stop for a bit will ultimately get back on track.

Twenty-five years ago, my friend Colin Hall and I tried to dispel those concerns by finding and interviewing as many students who took gap years as we could.

We profiled 33 of them in a book called *Taking Time Off*, which was published 20 years ago.

After news of Ms Obama's choice, I tracked down everyone from the book to see what had become of them.

Was their gap year ultimately incidental to their lives, or did it help them grow into the person they were meant to become? And for those who now had children, how would they react if their offspring wanted to take a gap year?

Families seeking data on gap years won't find much.

Part of the problem is that federal data on college delay and completion don't measure all the reasons people started college late.

While some people make a deliberate choice to delay college to serve in the military or work or travel, others meander for a few years before deciding to try college after all.

A number of researchers have shown a connection between a deliberate choice to take some time off and getting better grades upon return to the classroom.

Devin G. Pope, a professor of behavioral science also saw the link.

Bob Clagett, the former dean of admissions at Middlebury College, saw similar results when he helped inspire number-crunching among students there and at the University of North Carolina.

Once college is over, however, we enter the realm of anecdotal evidence when it comes to first jobs.

Parents worry that if their children take a gap year, they will appear wayward to employers, which may have more to do with the term than how that year was spent.

In fact, logic would suggest that many people who take a gap year get better jobs after college than people who don't.

If you were hiring entry-level employees, wouldn't you rather employ the risk-taking 23-year-olds who found their way in the world

for a while than the 22-year-olds who have not done much besides going to school?

该不该选择间隔年？
人生最大的冒险是不去冒险

文◎佚名

奥巴马的长女是一位十足的文化偶像，其衣着品位和走访高校的新闻经常登上头条。曾经一张疑似马莉娅，身穿印有布鲁克林嘻哈团体"进步时代"标识的T恤照片被人传出，结果令该团体创建者之一乔伊的维基百科页面访问量创下新高。还有人看到过马莉娅出现在HBO（美国家庭影院）出品的电视剧《衰姐们》的拍摄片场。据说她在给该剧制片人莉娜·杜汉姆（也是一位特立独行的美国物质女孩）当实习生。

如果你家十几岁的孩子说打算在高中和大学的间隙离开课堂一年，那很可能是拜马莉娅·奥巴马所赐。

但如果他们还没这样的想法,他们也该开始考虑要不要跟随她的脚步。

这位奥巴马小姐在去哈佛之前休学了。有些高中毕业生不知道自己想从大学里得到什么,或是希望按照学位课程安排所不允许的方案去找工作、旅行、做义工。因此像她那样,在高中升大学或是在本科阶段休学一段时间,这种做法对于他们来说非常有吸引力。

但是,这样的谈话往往会令父母担心。

如果十几岁的子女不想上学,没人会希望在他们身上投入六位数的求学费用。很多人怀疑,暂停学业一段时间的学生,最终还会不会回到求学的轨道上来。

在25年前,我和朋友科林·霍尔想尽可能地找寻并采访一些有过间隔年经历的学生,从而打消这些顾虑。

我们选了其中33个人做了深度报道,收录进一本名叫《休息一下》的书中,这本书在20年前出版。

在奥巴马大女儿的选择传出后,我追踪调查了那本书里的每个人,看看他们现在的状况。

他们的间隔年最终对人生没产生太大影响,还是的确帮助他们成长为自己想要成为的人?对那些现在有了孩子的人,如果他们的孩子想休学一年再上大学,他们会是什么反应?

很多家庭找不到太多关于间隔年的数据。

一个问题是，联邦的延迟上大学和毕业的数据并不涵盖人们延迟上大学的全部原因。

虽然有些人是有意延迟上大学，去参军、工作或旅行，也有些人只是晃荡了几年，才最终决定去上大学试试。

很多研究者发现，故意选择休学一段时间与回到学校后取得更好成绩之间存在联系。

芝加哥大学布斯商学院的行为学教授德温·G.波普也发现了这种联系。

米德尔伯里学院的前招生部主任鲍勃·克拉格特在帮助分析该校和北卡罗来纳大学的学生数据时也发现了类似的结果。

不过，一旦大学结束，开始第一份工作，这些案例就落入了轶事性经验证据的范畴。

父母们担心，如果孩子经历间隔年，雇主们会觉得他们太任性——这可能更多的是因为"间隔年"这个说法，而非这一年是如何度过的。

事实上，很多经历过间隔年的人在大学毕业后找到的工作，按道理应该比没经历过的人更好。

如果你在招聘初级职员，你会选择一个23岁的敢于冒险花一段时间在世界上寻找自己道路的人，还是一个22岁的除了上学没做过太多事情的人？ 绘英语

Proofreader Girl Kono Etsuko: A Boring Job Is So Great

文◎ Little J

  Etsuko dreams of becoming a fashion magazine editor. However, when finally entering a well-known publisher, she is assigned to the "Review Division", a super boring department. Even so, Etsuko is not discouraged. She dresses in flashy clothes every day with her pet phrase "Why". She meets authors in person and goes into actual locations to verify facts, going beyond her proofreading work. "Are you a loser if you can't achieve your dream?" "No, no matter what kind of job you are doing, you can get infinite pleasures if you dedicate yourself fully to it!"

《校对女孩河野悦子》：
无趣的工作，万岁

文◎小J 译◎小J

悦子的梦想是"成为时尚杂志的编辑"。当她终于进入一家知名出版社工作时，竟被派到超无趣的校阅部！即使如此也毫不气馁的悦子，每天身着超级花哨的时尚服装，她的口头禅是——"为什么"。悦子会自己去找作家见面，或为了追踪事件真相而卧底取材，工作大大超越了"校阅"的范畴。"不能实现梦想的人生就是失败的？""不，不管什么工作，只要全力去做，就能获得无穷的快乐！" 绘英语

Seventeen

文◎ Shiina Ringo

Now I'm seventeen

my school is in the country

students wear trainers

read the same magazines

Now I'm seventeen

my school is getting tiresome

teachers—they're so young

singling me out

only like philosophy

After school the time

that's what I call my own time

nice girls meet nice boys at the end of school day

while other girls go straight home

talking about soaps and that

I go home alone

watching the nameless people

surfing subways, travelling somewhere

"...nowhere..."

Now I'm seventeen, I do not have a title

depend on no one else

busy being king

I go home alone and have dinner in my sweet home

praying again, again & again

I see the same faces in school

they say that I am different
I think it's an honor
I say it's an honor to be different
I can't go their way
Now I'm seventeen
Now I'm seventeen

17 岁

文◎椎名林檎

现在我 17 岁
我的学校坐落于乡间
学生们脚穿运动跑鞋
翻看同一类杂志
现在我 17 岁
我的学校逐渐开始变得烦人
那些老师们——如此年轻
将我挑选出来
就像已成基本定律一般
放学后的时间
那才是我所谓的"私人时光"
美丽的女孩子们放学后与帅气的男孩子们约会去
其余的女孩子们径自回家
谈论着肥皂剧如何如何
我独自回家
看着身边匆匆而过的叫不上名的人们
在地下铁穿梭，去某处旅行

"……无处可去……"
现在我 17 岁，没什么头衔
也没有依靠任何人
整日忙着扮国王
我独自回家
然后在我那温馨的小家里吃晚饭
一遍遍地祈祷着
我看着学校里那些无异的脸庞
他们说我很不同
我将其视为一种光荣
我说让人觉得不同其实是一种光荣
我无法走和他们一样的路
现在我 17 岁
此刻我 17 岁

J.K. Rowing Is My Hero

文© Rachael

In July of 1965, Joanne Kathleen Rowling was born to the parents of Peter and Anne Rowling, little did they know that their daughter was going to grow up to be what many consider the author of the generation.

After attending Chepstow and Exeter University, J.K. Rowling traveled from her first real job in France back to London. On that delayed train she thought of the most marvelous idea she ever had: Harry Potter. After sitting on the train for four long hours, J.K. Rowling was finally able to get Harry Potter down on paper. That December, 1990, her mother died from multiple sclerosis. Anne Rowling had been battling the illness for quite some time. After six months of writing the first book, Rowling's first thought changed completely.

The death of her mother helped Rowling connect to her character. Harry's parents also died and Rowling could fully understand what her character would feel like. "Death became the central theme", Rowling said during an interview with Elizabeth Vargus. She also said that one of her biggest regrets was not telling her mother about *Harry Potter* before she died. Her mother would have loved the books and loved to know that her daughter was well off.

Desperate for a change, J.K. Rowling moved to Portugal and became an English teacher. There she got married and had her first child, Jessica. After leaving her husband of two years, Rowling and her daughter moved back to London.

This time in Rowling's life is her most depressing time. She struggled with clinical depression for many months. When ask about her depression in documentary "A Year in the Life,"she stated, "All color was drained out of my life." These moments in her life, gave life to the dementors in the *Harry Potter* series, terrible creatures that live off the misfortune of others. If you come across a dementor, they will drain all of the happiness from your soul. "We were as sick as you can be, without being homeless," J.K. Rowling stated earlier in the interview.

Not only was J.K. Rowling poor but she was trying to support her daughter, and write at the same time. Rowling would write while Jessica took naps in a small cafe. Finally after many months of writing, Rowling sent the final chapters of her first book to a small publisher in Britain. Little did she know that her life was about to change forever. "Harry turned my life around completely." Rowling said in the same interview with Elizabeth Vargus.

"Nine months after my mother's death, desperate to get away for a while, I left for Portugal. I took with me the still-growing manuscript of *Harry Potter*, hopeful that my new working hours (I taught in the afternoon and evening) would lend themselves to pressing on with my novel. The manuscript had changed a lot since my mother had died. Now, Harry's feelings about his dead parents had become much deeper; much stronger; much more real."

After *Harry Potter* was published in Britain J.K. Rowling received a call telling her that a *Harry Potter* bidding war was going on the United States. Scholastic bought *Harry Potter* and is the American publisher of the books. Astounded,Rowling finished her last sentence in the last book, *Harry Potter and the Deathly Hallows* and said, "So much expectation from the hard core fans, I am not sure I will ever be able to match up to it." She also said she was so lucky for having the idea. Fianlly, *Harry Potter* has been translated into 67 languages and on the first day the last book was on sale, books stores sold over 7,000 books per minute.

Harry Potter himself could be a hero to many people; however he is a fictional character. He was the boy that lived; Rowling was the girl that gave him life. I have always believed that a hero needs to be someone like no other. They must be brave and strong, courageous and bold. Superman for example was what I thought every hero should be like. J.K. Rowling doesn't save the world from the Joker or shoot webs out of her hands but she is brave, strong, courageous and bold.

J.K. Rowling is my hero because through her entire

life she never gave up on her ideas. She took events that happened in her life and made them part of her Harry Potter world. People always say things happen for a reason, well in J.K. Rowling's case things did happen for the right reason. If the train was not delayed then I would have had to find something to entertain me my whole childhood, much like *Harry Potter* did.

J.K. Rowling's life was far from perfect, she has lost contact with her father, she no longer has a mother, she is supporting three children and trying to give them a normal life when hers is so crazy. That is another reason for why J.K. Rowling is the perfect hero. She has a crazy life much like my own. Balancing school and sports and other after-school activities, sometimes I feel like I need to slow down. *Harry Potter* was my way to forget my own crazy life. I would get lost in the books for hours, reading until early morning. J.K. Rowling has the power to make people forget themselves and feel like they have no troubles in the world.

J.K. Rowling never gave up on *Harry Potter*, she wrote for her pleasure, not for what others wanted to read. Having such a hard core fan base can be very challenging. You want to keep them happy but more importantly you want to keep yourself happy and write a novel you can be proud of. J.K. Rowling is a primary example of how to do this. She killed favorite characters, changed locations and times, but she also made her readers happy.

In 2011, the final *Harry Potter* movie concluded, which meant *Harry Potter* was over. The final book was released in 2007, so there were no more movies to come. People lined the streets for hours to buy movie tickets, people waited at the premier in London for up to 8 days. J.K. imagined new

words, and stretched the boundaries of writing. She never stopped doing what she loves and she turned her idea into 7 incredible books and 8 great movies. The era that so many people loved is unfortunately ending. The books may be pushed to the back of the shelves, the movies may become less watched and the theme park may be less visited, but J.K. Rowling's imagination will always but remembered.

J.K. 罗琳是我的英雄

文◎ Rachael（蕾切尔）

1965年7月，在乔安娜·凯瑟琳·罗琳出生的时候，她的父母彼得·罗琳和安妮·罗琳绝对没有想到他们的女儿将会被很多人视为一代人最喜爱的作家。

在从切普斯托大学和埃克塞特大学毕业以后，她辞去自己的第一份工作，从法国回到英国。在那趟晚点的火车上，她想到了那个最绝妙的点子：哈利·波特。火车上漫长的四个小时以后，她终于让哈利·波特的形象出现在纸面上。同年，1990年12月，她的母亲安妮·罗琳因多发性硬化症去世。在此之前，母亲已经和病魔斗争了好长一段时间。这时，距离她开始写第一本书已经过去六个月，罗琳的想法发生了彻底的改变。

母亲的去世让她可以和书中的角色心灵相通。哈利的双亲也都早早离世，那时的罗琳完全能够理解她书中角色的感受。"死亡成为中心主题"，罗琳在伊丽莎白·瓦格斯的访谈中这样说道。她还说，在母亲去世以前，没有告诉她关于《哈利·波特》的一切是让她感到最遗憾的事情之一。她母亲会喜欢这些书，同时会为自己的女儿过得好而高兴。

渴望新生活的罗琳搬到了葡萄牙，成为了一名英语老师。在那儿，她结了婚，生下她的第一个孩子，杰西卡。两年以后，罗

琳离开了她的丈夫，和女儿搬回了伦敦。这段时间是她生活中的最低谷。她同临床忧郁症斗争了好几个月。后来，在纪录片《生命中最糟糕的一年》中，她说，"生命中所有的色彩都流干了"。这些糟糕的时刻，催生了《哈利·波特》系列中的摄魂怪——一种靠着其他人的不幸生存的怪物。如果你碰到了一个摄魂怪，它会把你灵魂中所有的快乐都吸走。她在早期的采访中说过这样一句话——"我们的生活曾经达到过你能想象的最糟糕的程度，差一点儿就无家可归。"

尽管生活窘迫，还要把孩子养大，她还是坚持了她的写作。罗琳会在杰西卡午睡的时候在小咖啡馆里写作。终于，在好几个月的辛苦工作之后，罗琳把第一本书的最后几章寄给了伦敦的一个小出版商。她不知道生活将从此永远改变。"哈利简直把我的生活调了个过儿"，罗琳在同一次采访中说道。

"母亲去世9个月后，我不顾一切地逃到了葡萄牙。我带上了未完成的《哈利·波特》手稿，希望我的新工作（我在下午和晚上授课）能给我时间继续完成我的小说。母亲离世后，我对手稿做了很大的改动。如今，哈利对于逝去双亲的感觉更加深刻，更加强烈，也更加真实了。"

《哈利·波特》在伦敦获得出版后，她接到了一个电话，通知她在美国将会有一场《哈利·波特》的出版权争夺大战。学者出版社最终买到了《哈利·波特》的版权，成为这一系列书的美国出版商。在震惊中，她完成了最后一本书《哈利·波特与死亡圣器》的最后一个句子。她说："铁杆粉丝的期望值太高，我不知道能不能达到他们的期望。"她还说，想出了那个主意她感到很幸运。最终，《哈利·波特》被译成67种文字，在最后一本书的首个销售日，书店每分钟卖出了7000多本书。

哈利·波特也许是很多人的英雄，然而他是小说中的一个形象。他是个幸存下来的男孩，罗琳是给他生命的女孩。我总是相信英雄应该是与众不同的。他们必须勇敢、坚强、有胆量。比如说超人就是我能想象到的所有英雄的缩影。J.K.罗琳没有把这个

世界从小丑和射击游戏中拯救出来,但是她同样既勇敢、坚强、又有胆量。

　　J.K.罗琳是我的英雄,因为在整个生命中,她从未放弃自己的想法。她把在自己生活中发生的事件放到了哈利·波特的世界中,让它们成为故事的一部分。人们常说事出有因,那么对于罗琳,事情的确由于恰当的原因而发生。如果没有火车延误,也许我就得再找其他东西来娱乐我的整个童年,就像《哈利·波特》那样。

　　罗琳的生活并不完美,她和父亲失去了联系,她没有了母亲,她抚养着三个孩子,并尽量给她们一个正常的生活,而她自己的生活已经如此疯狂。这就是我认为罗琳是个完美英雄的另一个原因。她有一个和我一样疯狂的生活。努力在学校、体育活动以及其他课外活动中获得平衡,有时我觉得自己应该放慢步伐。《哈利·波特》是我能够暂时忘记自己疯狂生活的一个方法。我会在书中沉迷好几个小时,一直读到清晨。J.K.罗琳有一种力量,能够让人们忘记自己,感到生活中没有任何烦恼。

　　J.K.罗琳从未放弃过《哈利·波特》。她为了自己的快乐而写作,而不是为了取悦读者。有这样一个铁杆粉丝团是一种非常严峻的挑战。你想让他们快乐,但更重要的是,你想让自己也感到快乐,写出一个自己能引以为傲的小说。J.K.罗琳自己就是如何能实现这一点的最佳例子。她杀掉了最受欢迎的角色,改变了故事的时间和地点,但她还是让她的读者们得到了快乐。

　　2011年,最后一部《哈利·波特》电影终结,这意味着《哈利·波特》时代的结束。最后一本书出版于2007年,所以将没有后续要拍摄的电影。人们排好几个小时的长队去买电影票,人们等了8天才等到伦敦的首映式。罗琳想出了新的词汇,扩展了写作的疆界。她从未放弃自己喜欢的事情,她把自己的想法变成了7部非凡的书和8部伟大的电影。那么多人钟爱的一个时代无奈地结束了。那些书可能会被束之高阁,那些电影可能不再有那么多人看,那个主题公园可能不再有那么多人去参观,但是J.K.罗琳的非凡想象会永远留在人们的记忆深处。

Emma Watson:
You Can Be a Warrior

文◎ anonymous

  Emma Watson entered our lives as the perfect Hermione Granger in 2001, now we're just as much in love with this charming, intelligent British, as ever. You may or may not be a Potter head, but there's nobody on this planet (no, we're not exaggerating) who is not charmed by the perfection that is Emma Watson.
  Despite achieving stardom at the young age of 11, she's never gone the Hollywood spoiled child route. In fact, she made all attempts to stay as "normal" as possible. She

said, "Ignoring fame was my rebellion. I was insistent on being normal and doing normal things. It probably wasn't advisable to go to college in America and room with a complete stranger. And it probably wasn't wise to share a bathroom with eight other people in a coed dorm. Looking back, that was crazy."

She also works really hard. She said, "I was very well-educated. My dad paid for me to go to a very good school, but, you know, when my parents divorced, we didn't have any money for a while. And so I worked hard every single day that I was at that school to make him proud of me and for him to know that I appreciated it. And I do, and I still do."

If we had to imagine what Hermione Granger would have grown up to be like, we would say she'd be the Emma Watson of the wizarding world, because there really is no way to separate the two. Much like her famous persona on screen, in the last few years, Emma has added more feathers to her cap than we could imagined. Actor, scholar, model, UN Women Goodwill Ambassador. In her role of the UN Women Goodwill Ambassador, she's supported powerful causes to the best of her ability and brought them all the attention they deserve.

We might never know where Hermione Granger ends and Emma Watson begins. She gave us the most accurate description of our favourite girl from the Potter universe. "Young girls are told you have to be a delicate princess. Hermione taught them that you can be a warrior."

艾玛·沃特森：
你可以成为战士

译◎阿诺

2001年，艾玛·沃特森以完美的赫敏·格兰杰的形象走进了我们的生活。如今，我们对这个迷人而充满智慧的英国女孩依然爱之如故。无论你是不是《哈利·波特》迷，这个世界上没有一个人（不，我们并不是在夸大其词）不为艾玛·沃特森这个完美的女孩着迷。

尽管年仅11岁就成了明星，她并未走上被惯坏了的好莱坞小孩儿的道路。事实上，她尽一切努力使自己尽可能地保持"普通"。她曾说："无视名气就是我表达叛逆的有趣方式。我坚持当个普通人，做普通的事。去美国上大学，还和一个完全不认识的人当室友，这或许并不可取。在男女混合宿舍跟另外八个人共用一间浴室或许也不明智。回过头去看，当时的做法真是疯狂。"

她还格外努力。她说："我从小受到很好的教育。爸爸出钱供我读一所非常好的学校，可是，你知道的，当我的父母离婚后，有一段时间我们没有钱。因此，在那所学校的每一天我都非常努力，为的是让他为我骄傲，让他知道我很感激他。我现在也很努力，仍然在努力。"

如果非要让我们想象赫敏·格兰杰长大后会是什么样，我们会说她会成为魔法世界里的艾玛·沃特森，因为实在无法把她们两个人分割开。与她在银幕上塑造的那个众所周知的角色很相似，在过去的几年中，艾玛所取得的引以为豪的成就比我们所能想象的还要多。她是演员、学者、模特，还是联合国妇女亲善大使。在联合国妇女亲善大使的岗位上，她竭尽所能支持那些有影响力

的运动,为它们争取到应有的关注。

  我们或许永远也无法将赫敏·格兰杰和艾玛·沃特森截然分开。对于《哈利·波特》世界中这个我们最喜欢的女孩,她给了我们最准确的描述:"人们告诉年轻女孩,你们要做娇贵的公主。而赫敏却教会她们,你可以成为战士。" 绘英语

一个镜头，数张写真，讲述的是一个国家、一个民族的故事。

Chen Man: Changing How the World Sees China

文◎ anonymous

As China becomes increasingly important in the world of fashion, one photographer is leading the scene — 35-year-old Beijing native Chen Man.

Firmly established as the country's go-to fashion photographer, her work has featured across a range of leading publications, including *Vogue*, *Elle*, *Harper's Bazaar*, *Cosmopolitan* and *i.D*.

Nor is her fame limited to within China.

As well as shooting a veritable A-to-Z list of Chinese celebrities, international stars such as Sophie Marceau, Rihanna, Nicole Kidman and Victoria Beckham have also posed for her.

CNN Style pays a visit to Chen Man's studio in downtown Beijing, as she prepares to shoot back-to-back spreads of famous actresses Fan Bingbing and Shu Qi.

Chen's work is immediately identifiable. Highly-stylized through the use of modern post-production techniques, and incorporating a range of eastern themes and iconography, her shoots can be viewed as representative of a new aspirational China.

During her meeting with CNN Style, Chen discusses the continuing influence of her childhood in Beijing, and how growing up in the city's hutongs during a time when food was sparse in the winter, neighbors lived in close quarters, and space was communal, has shaped her outlook on life.

Like her peers, Chen has witnessed enormous change in Beijing, and has sought to document the profound effect those changes have had on her generation.

Her craft has spanned the wide range of magazine covers, commercial shoots, fine art photography and extends to other modes of expression, such as her lesser-known traditional paintings.

陈漫：
改变外国人看待中国的方式

译◎阿诺

由于中国在时尚界的地位变得越来越重要，一位摄影师成为了台前幕后的主角，她就是35岁的北京人陈漫。

作为中国时尚界资深的摄影师，陈漫的作品登上过一系列主流出版物，包括 Vogue Elle《时尚芭莎》《时尚·COSMOPOLITAN》和 i-D。

她的名气不限于中国。

陈漫不但为一大串中国名人拍过照，苏菲·玛索、蕾哈娜、妮可·基德曼和维多利亚·贝克汉姆等国际明星也曾为她摆过造型。

CNN Style（美国有线电视新闻网风格频道）走访了位于北京市中心的陈漫工作室，当时她正准备为著名女演员范冰冰和舒淇拍摄背对背写真。

陈漫的作品辨识度很高。通过使用当代后期制作技术，广泛地融合东方主题和肖像画，她的摄影作品代表了一个全新的具有宏图伟志的中国。

在与 CNN Style 会面时，陈漫讨论了她在北京度过的童年以及在北京胡同里长大的故事对她产生的持久影响。那时在冬天食物很少，邻居们住得很近，空间也是公用的，这些都塑造了她的人生观。

与同龄人一样，陈漫见证了北京的巨大变化，并寻求记录这些变化对她这代人产生的深远影响。

她的作品遍布各大杂志封面、商业摄影、美术摄影，并延伸至其他的表达模式，例如更少为人知的传统绘画。

Lady Gaga（嘎嘎小姐）在"周末清晨"采访中诉说了出名的烦恼，称怀念自己与别人正常交往的时光。

Lady Gaga Talks about the Downsides of Fame

文© anonymous

The pop star, who made a name for herself by dressing up in outrageous outfits in public, got candid as she spoke about the lack of privacy she experiences as soon as she steps out her front door.

"I'm very acutely aware that once I cross that property line I'm not free anymore. As soon as I go out into the world, I belong, in a way, to everyone else," she said to CBS's Lee Cowan. "It's legal to follow me. It's legal to stalk me at the beach. And I can't call the police or ask them to leave."

"Well, if I can't be free out there, I can be free in here," Gaga explained, pointing to her chest.

    The singer also spoke about how much she misses regular, everyday human interactions.

    "I miss people," the artist said as she began to tear up. "I miss, you know, going anywhere and meeting a random person and saying 'Hi,' and having a conversation about life. I love people."

    The 30-year-old spoke about fame's negative side earlier, saying, "I don't think I could think of a single thing that's more isolating than being famous," during a discussion with Jamie Lee Curtis for *Variety* magazine.

    Gaga also told *The Guardian* in 2013 she used to hide in her house "to preserve my image as a superstar to my fans."

    "I don't mean I am a superstar, I mean that they only ever see me at my best," she said. "And it really drove me crazy."

出名真的好吗？
Lady Gaga 告诉你

译◎ Yaki（亚琪）

这位流行音乐歌手以在公共场合穿着搞怪惊人而出名。不过，在视频中她开诚布公，直言自己一出门就没有隐私权。

"我很清楚，一旦我走出家门就失去自由身了。一走出来，我在某种程度上就属于公众了，"她对CBS（哥伦比亚广播公司）的Lee Cowan（李·考思）说道，"跟着我是合法的，在海滩上跟踪我也是合法的。我还不能报警或赶走他们。"

Gaga指着自己的胸口继续说道："既然在外面我没法自由自在，那我就在心里放松一下。"

这位歌手也坦言自己多么怀念与人正常交往的时光。

"我很想念人群，" Gaga抹着泪说道，"我非常想念那种

无论走到哪儿，随便见到别人都可以打个招呼，和他们谈谈生活琐事的日子。我很喜欢人群。"

这位30岁的歌手在早些时候也谈到出名的负面影响，"我已经找不到任何比出名还令人孤独的事了"，这是她在《综艺》杂志上与Jamie Lee Curtis（杰米·李·柯蒂斯）的一段谈话。

Gaga也曾于2013年对《卫报》称，自己曾一度躲在家里，以便"维持自己在粉丝心中的巨星形象"。

她说："我不是炫耀自己是明星，我只想让他们看到我最好的一面，这简直要把我逼疯了。"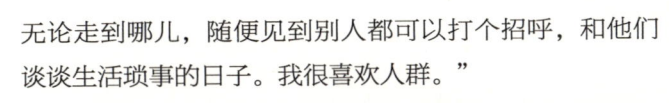

Take Your Broken Heart, Make It into Art

文◎ Meryl Streep

Thank you Hollywood Foreign Press. Just to pick up on what Hugh Laurie said, you and all of us in this room, belong to the most vilified segment in American society right now. Think about it: Hollywood, foreigners, and the press. But, who are we? And what is Hollywood, anyway? Just a bunch of people from other places.

I was born and raised and educated in the public schools of New Jersey. Viola Davis was born in a sharecroppers' cabin in South Carolina, came up in Central Falls, RhodeIsland. Sarah Paulson was born in Florida, raised by a single mom in Brooklyn. Sarah Jessica Parker was one of seven or eight kids from Ohio. Amy Adams was born in Vicenza, Italy. And Natalie Portman was born in Jerusalem. Where are their birth certificates? And the beautiful Ruth Negga was born in Addis Ababa, Ethiopia, raised in Ireland. And she's here nominated for playing a small-town girl from Virginia.

Ryan Gosling, like all the nicest people, is Canadian. And Dev Patel was born in China, raised in London, and is here playing an Indian raised in Tasmania. So Hollywood is crawling with outsiders and foreigners. And if we kick them all out, we'll have nothing to watch but football and mixed martial arts, which are not the arts.

An actor's only job is to enter the lives of people who are different from us and let you feel what that feels like. And there are many, many, many powerful performances this year that did exactly that. Breathtaking, compassionate work.

But there was one performance this year that stunned me, sank a hook in my heart. Not because it was good. There was nothing good about it. But it was effective and it did its job. It made its intended audience laugh and show their teeth. It was that moment when the person asking to sit in the most respected seat in our country imitated a disabled reporter.

Someone he outranked in privilege, power. It kind of broke my heart when I saw that. I still can't get it out of my head because it wasn't in a movie. It was real life. And this instinct to humiliate when it's modeled by someone in the public platform, by someone powerful, filters down into everyone's life because it kind of gives permission for other people to do the same thing. Disrespect invites disrespect. Violence incites violence. And when the powerful use their position to bully others, we all lose.

This brings me to the press. We need the principled press to hold power to account. That's why our founders enshrined the press and its freedoms in our constitution. So, I only ask the famously Hollywood Foreign Press and all of us in our community to join me in supporting the committee to support journalists. Because we're going to need them going forward and they're going to need us to safeguard the truth.

    One more thing: Once when I was standing around on the set one day, whining about something, you know, we were going to work through supper, Tommy Lee Jones said to me, "Isn't it such a privilege, Meryl, just to be an actor?" Yeah, it is. And we have to remind each other of the privilege and the responsibility of the act of empathy. We should all be very proud of the work Hollywood honors here today. As my friend, the dear departed Princess Leia said to me once, "Take your broken heart, make it into art." Thank you.

本文为好莱坞女演员梅丽尔·斯特里普在第74届金球奖上的演讲。

带着你的破碎之心，去创造艺术吧

文◎ Meryl Streep（梅丽尔·斯特里普）

谢谢你们，好莱坞海外记者协会。接着休·劳瑞的话说，你和我们都在这间屋子里，同属于当下美国社会最易为人所诟病的一角。想想看：好莱坞、外国人、记者。但是，我们是谁？以及，好莱坞是什么？不过是一帮外来人罢了。

我出生、成长、受教育于新泽西的公立学校。维奥拉·戴维斯出生于南加州的农村小屋，在罗德岛的大瀑布脚下成长。莎拉·保罗森在佛罗里达出生，在布鲁克林由一位单身妈妈带大。莎拉·杰西卡·帕克是俄亥俄一个有七八个孩子的家庭中的一员。艾米·亚当斯出生于意大利的维琴察。娜塔莉·波特曼出生于耶路撒冷。他们的出生证明在哪儿呢？美丽的鲁丝·内伽出生于埃塞俄比亚的亚的斯亚贝巴，在爱尔兰长大。而她现在却因扮演一个弗吉尼亚的小镇姑娘被提名。

瑞恩·高斯林，像所有友善的人一样，是加拿大人。而戴夫·帕特尔则生于中国、长于伦敦，出演一位在塔斯马尼亚长大的印度人。所以好莱坞满是外来人和外国人。如果我们把他们全赶出去，那除了橄榄球和综合格斗以外，我们再无其他东西可看，而这些东西连艺术都不是。

演员的唯一工作就是进入那些异于自己的人的生活中，让你知道那些不同的生活是什么样的。而今年，许许多多震撼人心的表演也确实做到了。多么伟大却又充满悲悯的工作啊。

但今年，有一场表演令我震惊。它深深地勾住了我的心。不是因为表演有多出色。它没什么值得称道的。但它很有效，而且做到了它想做的事。它使自己的目标观众露齿大笑了。那就是当

一个要坐在我们国家最受尊敬之位的人,模仿嘲笑一位残疾记者的时候。

那个人,他居于特权、权力的高位。我看到那个场景时有些心碎。它在我脑海中挥之不去,因为那不是电影。那是真实发生的事。当这些行为被某个有影响力的人搬上公共舞台时,那种羞辱的本能就渗入每个人的生活中,因为这像是允许别人做同样的事。不敬带来不敬。暴力催生暴力。当有权势的人利用职位之便来欺凌他人时,我们全都输得一败涂地。

这又让我说到媒体。我们需要有原则的记者来掌握话语权。这正是我们的国父们将记者和新闻自由写入宪法的原因。所以,我谨邀请闻名遐迩的好莱坞海外记者协会,以及这个圈子里的所有人和我一起,来支持这个协会,也就是支持记者们。因为我们需要他们开辟前路,而他们需要我们来维护真相。

还有一件事:有一次,我正站在片场抱怨着什么——你懂的,我们经常因工作吃不了晚饭——汤米·李·琼斯跟我说:"这难道不是一种特别的荣幸吗,梅丽尔,当演员?"没错,是的。而我们也要彼此提醒,这种荣幸,以及我们让大家产生共鸣的责任。我们都应该自豪于好莱坞今天给予荣誉的作品。正如我的朋友,已逝的莉亚公主对我说的那般"带着你破碎的心,去创造艺术吧。"谢谢。 疯英语

What Did You Done to the Girls When You Ask Them to Be Pretty, Small, and Quiet

文◎ Lisa Capretto

When she was a little girl, best-selling author Glennon Doyle Melton was often described as "pretty" or "adorable." People commented on her childhood beauty, and strangers were drawn in by her smile. But when a young Glennon would speak to these adults with confidence and clarity, she sensed them pulling back.

As Glennon writes in her memoir, "Love Warrior", she was about 10 years old when the disturbing realization hit her: "I begin to understand that beauty warms people, and smart cools people." It's a passage that stands out to Oprah, who asks the author about it when the two sit down for a conversation aired on "SuperSoul Sunday." Glennon begins by describing society's expectation for girls and how it influences their psyche. "I think the world wants girls to be pretty and small and quiet," she says. "As long as I was able to stay pretty and small and quiet, everything would be fine."

Glennon, who has since become celebrated for her candor and openness, points out that society's indoctrination of girls sets them up for failure. "How can you be a successful girl if the purpose of being human and growing is. to find your voice?" she asks. "It's a set-up."

当你要求女生娇小可人
又文静的时候，她们遭受了什么

文◎ Lisa Capretto（丽莎·卡普雷托）

当畅销书作家格蕾侬·道尔·梅尔顿还是个小女孩的时候，常常被形容成"漂亮""可爱"。熟悉她的人赞叹她的美丽娇小，不熟悉她的人则沉醉于她迷人的微笑。当年轻的格蕾侬拥有了自己的思想，自信且观点鲜明地与这些成年人交谈时，她感到他们有些敬而远之。

她在回忆录《爱的战士》中写道：美丽让人靠近，睿智让人疏远。这是10岁时经历的现实带给她的深刻记忆。这篇文章引起了Oprah（奥普拉）的重视，在一次直播访谈类节目"Supersuper soul Soul Sunday（《超级灵魂星期日》）"中，她俩促膝长谈。格蕾侬说受世俗的影响，女孩们的心理会产生变化。"所有人对于女孩的期望就是：漂亮、娇小、矜持。只要我能够做到这些，那么就会被世界温柔相待。"

此后，格蕾侬因她的坦言、率真而被人称道，她指出社会对女孩们因循守旧的教条让女孩们很难成功。"在你的生活和成长过程中，如果仅仅一份话语权就需要你去奋斗才能得到，那你怎么可能成功？"她质问道，"这是一个圈套。"

在央视节目《中国诗词大会》第二季上,来自复旦附中的一名00后学生武亦姝分外抢眼,她以丰富的古诗词储备最终获得冠军,不少网友都被她的才情所折服。

Wu Yishu Wins *Chinese Ancient Poetry Competition* and Lots of Fans

文◎ Tao Xiangfei

Wu Yishu, a student at the High School Affiliated to Fudan University in Shanghai, beat other competitors in the second season of the Chinese Poetry Conference on China Central Television on Feb 7.

"I get feelings from ancient poetry that modern people cannot give me. I pay little attention to the competition result, but I love poetry, and it is enough as long as I enjoy the happiness brought by the poetry." Wu said.

In the final, Wu performed strongly in many sections, such as recalling poems by looking at sand paintings and reciting poems as many as she could think of relating to the Chinese character "Jiu," meaning liquor.

As early as Feb 1, when Wu recited an ancient Chinese

poem about the months of the year, the judges estimated that Wu must have remembered at least more than 2,000 Chinese ancient works.

Wu's strong performance in the Chinese ancient rhythm works earned her many fans and inspired others to learn ancient works.

The 1.8-meter tall Wu said that she kept only one ancient poetry book on bookshelves at her dormitory room instead of other books such as math, physics and chemistry books that her classmates have kept on their bookshelves.

She is known among her classmates and teachers as she loves reading poetry and wearing ancient Chinese clothes.

Zhou Hong, a professor from the Department of Chinese language and literature of East China Normal University, said that he had read some of the girl's poetry in 2015, and had published some on his blog.

武亦姝夺冠《中国诗词大会》，圈粉无数

文◎陶祥飞

武亦姝是上海复旦附中的学生，在2月7日央视节目《中国诗词大会》第二季上击败了所有参赛者，成功夺冠。

武亦姝说道:"我从古诗中得到了一种现代人无法给予我的感觉。我对比赛结果并不太在意,但我喜欢诗歌,只要能够享受诗歌带来的乐趣,于我而言就已经足够了。"

在决赛环节,武亦姝在许多方面的表现都非常抢眼,比如看沙画来回忆古诗,尽其所能背诵与"酒"有关的古诗。

早在2月1日,武亦姝背诵了一首有关月份的古诗,当时评委估计称武亦姝能背诵的古诗储量至少在2000首以上。

武亦姝在古诗词方面的出色表现圈了一大票粉丝,也激励了许多人去学习古代诗词。

这位身高1.8米的姑娘说,跟她的同学书架上都摆满了数理化书籍不同,她宿舍的书架上只有一本古诗书籍。

由于喜欢读古代诗词、穿古代服装,武亦姝在老师和同学们中名气很大。

华东师范大学中国语言文学系教授周虹表示说,2015年他读过武亦姝的一些诗词,还在自己的博客上发表了一些。绘英语

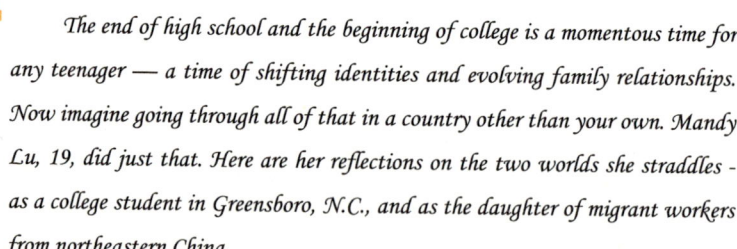

A Girl Between Two Worlds

文◎ Mandy Lu

The end of high school and the beginning of college is a momentous time for any teenager — a time of shifting identities and evolving family relationships. Now imagine going through all of that in a country other than your own. Mandy Lu, 19, did just that. Here are her reflections on the two worlds she straddles - as a college student in Greensboro, N.C., and as the daughter of migrant workers from northeastern China.

A couple of months ago, I went back to China for the first time since before I started college in the U.S.. It was my first trip home in two years.

When I saw my parents and grandmother at the airport, I felt awkward. I didn't really know what to say to them.

The first thing my mother said to me is, "You're not

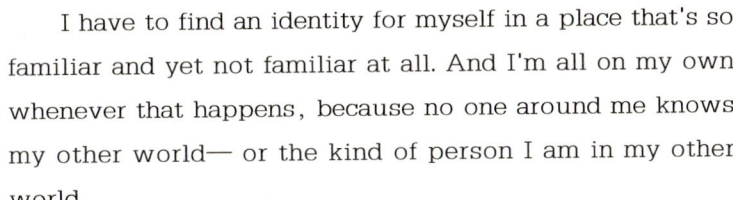

fat." She always tells me I've gained weight when I talk to her over Skype.

Whenever I cross the border between my two worlds, for the first few days, I feel like I'm in a daze.

I have to find an identity for myself in a place that's so familiar and yet not familiar at all. And I'm all on my own whenever that happens, because no one around me knows my other world— or the kind of person I am in my other world.

My parents are from northeastern China. They're migrant workers, living in Beijing. Financially, they're not very stable. They run a traditional medicine shop doing acupuncture and massage. They work seven days a week. I look at how hard their lives are, and I feel guilty that I can't help.

It's hard for them to get a grip on what things are like for me. I don't think they know enough about America to have the capacity to understand certain things. Like how

I don't eat steamed buns for breakfast at school. Or how I could disagree with my professor. Or why a dance party at college where everybody cross-dresses is fun.

So we end up talking about mundane subjects like what I want to eat for lunch.

On my trip home, I spent a lot of time sitting around with family eating or just snacking on sunflower seeds. My parents think it's important for me to connect with my relatives. But I have almost nothing to say. Sometimes I wonder if I'm actually related to them.

As conversations at the dinner table would get louder and louder, I would have flashbacks to the racket my friends and I would make in the cafeteria over someone's silly trick with a straw, or the racket we'd make with test tubes and beakers in the chemistry lab. I found myself missing all of that.

At the same time, seeing where my relatives live was a reminder of my roots.

This past year at school, I lived in a standard freshman double. The room was about the size of the place where my whole family of three plus my grandmother used to live. Many of my college friends complained about our dorm. But for me, it felt like a really safe and comfortable place to be.

I have been back from my visit to China for two months now. I'm still debating whether I should put pictures from my trip on Facebook. Here in the U.S., I've been unconsciously only putting my "American" self out there. Maybe I'm afraid to show my differences. Or maybe I'm simply avoiding the many questions I know will come my way.

行走在两个世界的女孩

文◎ Mandy Lu（曼迪·卢）

  对于任何一个十七八岁的孩子来说，从高中毕业到大学伊始都是一个关键时期。这段时间里，孩子的自我认同感和与家人的关系逐渐发生变化。此刻请想象一下，在异国他乡经历上述事情的情景。19岁的Mandy Lu（曼迪·卢）已经开始经历这些了。Mandy是美国北卡罗来纳州格林斯伯勒学院的学生，她的父母是来自中国东北的打工者。以下是她对自己行走在两个世界的思考。

  几个月前，我第一次回国，在美国读大学之前我从未回去过，这是我两年来的首次返乡之旅。

  当我在机场看到我的父母和奶奶时，我感到无所适从。我真的不知道该对他们说些什么。

  我妈对我说的第一句话是"你不胖"。我们在Skype（网络电视）上通话时她总是说我长胖了。

  无论何时每当我跨越两个世界的边界，最初的几天我都会觉得晕乎乎的。

  在一个既十分熟悉又完全陌生的地方，我必须找到自己的定位。每当此时我只能自求多福，因为我周围没有一个人了解我的另一个世界，也没有人了解另一个世界里的我。

  我的父母来自中国东北，目前在北京打工，经济收入并不稳定。他们经营着一家中药店，从事针灸和按摩，每周工作七天。看到他们生活如此艰辛，而我却爱莫能助，我便感到心存愧疚。

  我的父母很难理解我眼中的世界是个什么样子。我觉得他们对美国知之甚少，以至于无法明白那里发生的某些事情。比如：他们不理解在学校吃早餐怎么可以不吃包子，或者我竟然敢与教授的意见相左，又或为何我觉得在校园舞会上男女易服（女扮男装或男扮女装）很有趣。

  每每至此，我们的谈话通常会以"我中午想吃什么"这样的一些日常琐事而告终。

  这次回家探亲，很多时候我就是和家人坐在一起吃吃饭或者嗑嗑瓜子。我父母认为和亲戚保持联系很重要。然而，面对亲人们我几乎无话可说。有时我会想，我真的和他们有什么亲缘关系吗？

  当饭桌上的交谈声一浪高过一浪，我的耳畔就回响起和朋友在食堂里的嬉笑声，在那里我们看到有人用吸管滑稽地耍把戏；抑或听到化学实验室里试管和烧杯相互碰撞，叮当作响。我发现自己十分想念那些。

  与此同时，亲戚们居住的地方又提醒着我自己从何处来。我的姑姑们至今仍然住在北京郊外一带打工人员聚居的地方。

  在过去的一学年里，我住的是专门为新生准备的标准双人间，这间屋子足有过去我们一家三口外加我奶奶住的那间屋子大小。我的许多外国朋友对学校的住宿条件颇有微词，但是，对我而言，这里简直可以称得上一个安适的居所。

  现在，我已经回到美国两个月了。对于是否将这次探亲之旅所拍摄的照片上传到Facebook（脸谱网）上，我仍然犹豫不决。在美国，我一直下意识地只把"美国的我"张贴在那里，我也许是害怕暴露自己的与众不同，抑或我仅是在回避那些迟早要出现在我面前的问题。

此文为蕾哈娜在哈佛大学的演讲,话语动人心弦。

If You've Got a Dollar, There's Plenty to Share

文◎ Rihanna

When I was five or six years old, I remember watching TV and I would see these commercials, and I was watching other children suffer in other parts of the world and you know the commercials were like, "you can give 25 cents, save a child's life". And I would think to myself like, I wonder how many 25 cents I could save up to save all the kids in Africa. And I would say to myself, "when I grow up, when I can get rich, I'll save kids all over the world." I just didn't know I would be in the position to do that by the time I was a teenager.

At 17 I started my career here in America, and by the age of 18, I started my first charity organization. I went on to team up with other organizations in the following years and met, helped, and even lost some of the most beautiful souls. We're all human. And we all just want a chance: a chance at life, a chance in education, a chance at a future, really.

People make it seem way too hard. The truth is, and what I want the little girl watching those commercials to

know, is you don't have to be rich to be a humanitarian. You don't have to be rich to help somebody. You don't gotta be famous. You don't even have to be college-educated.

But it starts with your neighbour, the person right next to you, the person sitting next to you in class, the kid down the block in your neighbourhood, you just do whatever you can to help in any way that you can. And today I want to challenge each of you to make a commitment to help one person, one organization, one situation that touches your heart. My grandmother always used to say, "If you've got a dollar, there's plenty to share." Thank you ladies and gentlemen. It was my honour.

你只要有一美元，就有很多东西可以分享

文◎ Rihanna（蕾哈娜）　译◎杨鹏

五六岁的时候，我记得看电视我会看这些商业广告，我看到世界其他地方的孩子们经历的不幸，你知道商业广告就是"如果你献出25分钱，那么就可以拯救一个孩子的生命"。我会自己这样想，我想我能够存下多少个25分钱来拯救非洲的所有孩子。我会对自己说，"当我长大时，我富裕了，我要拯救全世界的孩子"。我只是没想到我在十几岁的时候就这样做了。

17岁的时候，我在美国开始了自己的事业，18岁的时候，我成立了自己的首个慈善机构。在接下来几年里，我继续与其他组织合作，我们遇见、帮助，甚至是失去过一些最为美丽的灵魂。我们都是人。我们都想有个机会：一个生活的机会，一个接受教育的机会，一个把握未来的机会，真的。

人们让这个看起来很难。事实上,我希望那些看商业广告的小孩儿知道的是,成为一个人道主义者,你不一定要多富有。帮助别人不一定得腰缠万贯。你不必声名远播,甚至不必接受过大学教育。

帮助别人从你的身边人做起,现在在你旁边的人、教室里坐在你旁边的人、邻居的孩子,你可以尽你所能用一切方法去帮助他们。今天,我希望你们每一个人都能承诺,在触动内心的时候,去帮助身边需要帮助的每一个人,去协助每一个需要帮助的组织机构更好地运转。我的祖母过去常说,"如果你有一美元,那么你就有很多东西来分享"。女士们、先生们,谢谢你们。这是我的荣幸。绘英语

Dreamlike Childhood

文◎ Xie Wanying

Whenever she looks back on the past, her childhood always seems to be a mere dream! How in those days it used to fill her heart with great pleasure to find herself the very picture of magnificent beauty when, clad in a gold-threaded naval uniform and armed with a saber at her waist, she ambled along with a loose rein on a giant of a white horse, little knowing that she would someday be reduced to being a solitary writer wielding the pen to depict her dreams and emotions!

She was always dressed like a male child until she was ten. Before that, her father would often take her with him when he attended dinner parties arranged for the recreation of servicemen. Her father's friends, the moment they saw her, would praise her by saying, "What a heroic little soldier! How old are you now?" Her father would end up the small talk smilingly with, "She's my son as well as my daughter."

She learned how to beat the drum for soldiers marching in parade and blow the bugle for fall-in. She was familiar with the mechanism of a Mauser. She also knew how to feed a big shell into the barrel of a cannon. True, the five to six years of military training she received inadvertently by the side of her father ended up in making a sprightly little soldier of her.

And what's more, she didn't share the same likes with ordinary girls. That was nothing unusual because, being the only little girl in the neighborhood, she had no female

playmates at all. Occasionally she caught glimpses of some young country girls, dressed in bright green or red and with bound feet, trudging past below the mountain. But she had no way of knowing their day-to-day life, and nor did she give much thought to what she saw. The saber, the horse — that was what she would like to have for lifelong company. Things about young females — how trivial and boring they seemed to her!

With the boundless expanse of the ocean gleaming coldly now here and now there under the radiance of the searchlight, steadfast naval officers, standing in two rows under the light and flag, would solemnly raise their glasses in unison to drink to their motherland amidst the rattle of sabers. Fancy the very scene moving her to copious tears of joy!

Soon it was about time for her to wake up from the dream! After all, life is a dream, isn't it?After she returned to her native place at the age of ten, she began to dress like a girl and, through associating with her young female relatives, gradually learned the girlish ways of thinking and behavior. For instance, silk thread of all colors was fancied for beautiful needle work; fragrant brilliant flowers should be put in hair for decoration; dressing should be followed by taking a look in a mirror; when sitting among a crowd, a girl should speak in a soft and delicate tone; she should be lachrymose and normally somewhat petulant like a pampered child.

The new surroundings, however, were also conducive to her upbringing. But the saber, given her by her father, was still hanging by her window. She would be struck by its cold gleam whenever she unsheathed it. Ah, the

white horse, the seashore, the soldiers carrying rifles on their shoulders. How the vague memories would bring her infinite anxiety and sadness! When her young female relatives called to her from outside the window, she would refuse to leave her room. She would instead stand inside for hours, nostalgic tears trickling down in drops.

Now what the ten unforgettable years has left her is a strong character. She is still fond of watching soldiers march in step and hearing the solemn and stirring call of a bugle. Nay, that's not what she is so much fond as afraid of watching. Whether wielding a sword on galloping horse or holding a pen in deep thought, she is the same person. Only time has made all the difference... Childhood! It's an indelible dream, isn't it?

文◎冰心　译◎张培基

　　她回想起童年的生涯，真是如同一梦罢了！穿着黑色带金线的军服，佩着一柄短短的军刀，骑在很高大的白马上，在海岸边缓辔徐行的时候，心里只充满了壮美的快感，几曾想到现在的自己，是这般静寂，只拿着一枝笔，写她幻想中的情绪呢？

　　十岁前，她总是穿得像个男孩子。在这之前，她父亲常常带她去参与那军人娱乐的宴会。朋友们一见都夸奖说，"好英武的一个小军人！今年几岁了？"父亲先一面答应着，临走时才微笑说，"他是我的儿子，但也是我的女儿。"

　　她会打走队的鼓，会吹召集的喇叭。知道毛瑟枪里的机关。

也会将很大的炮弹旋进炮腔里。当然，这五六年在父亲身边无形中接收的军事训练真将她培养成很矫健的小军人了。

别的方面呢？平常女孩子所喜好的事，她却一点儿都不爱。这也难怪她，她的四围并没有别的女伴，偶然看见山下经过的几个村里的小姑娘，穿着大红大绿的衣裳，裹着很小的脚。匆匆一面里，她无从知道她们平居的生活。而且她也不把这些印象放在心上。一把刀，一匹马，便堪过尽一生了！女孩子的事，是何等的琐碎烦腻啊！

当探海的电灯射在浩浩无边的大海上，发出一片一片的寒光，灯影下，旗影下，两排沉豪英毅的军官在剑佩锵锵的声里，整齐严肃地一同举起杯来，祝中国万岁的时候，这光景，是怎样使人涌出慷慨快乐的眼泪的呢？

她这梦也应当到了醒觉的时候了！人生就是一梦吗？十岁回到故乡去，换上了女孩子的衣服，在姊妹群中，学到了女儿情性：五色的丝线，是能做成好看的活计的；香的，美丽的花，是要插在头上的；镜子是妆束完时要照一照的；在众人中间坐着，是要说些很细腻很温柔的话的；眼泪是时常要落下来的。女孩子是总有点儿脾气，带点儿娇贵的样子的。

这也是很新颖，很能造就她的环境——但她父亲送给她的那把佩刀还长日挂在窗前。拔出鞘来，寒光射眼，她每每呆住了。白马啊，海岸啊，荷枪的军人啊……模糊中有无穷的怅惘。姊妹们在窗外唤她，她也不出去了。站了半天，只掉下几滴无聊的眼泪。

十年深刻的印象，遗留于她现在的生活中的，只是矫强的性质了——她依旧是喜欢看那整齐的步伐，听那悲壮的军笳。但与其说她是喜欢看，喜欢听，不如说她是怕看，怕听罢。横刀跃马和执笔沉思的她，原都是一个人，然而时代将这些事隔开了……童年！只是一个深刻的梦吗？绘英语

提到艾玛·沃特森（Emma Watson），你可能会想到那个一头蓬蓬卷发的小魔女"赫敏"，或者那个从常青藤大学毕业的学霸美少女。不过今天，我们要关注一下她作为联合国妇女亲善大使（UN Women Goodwill Ambassador）所做的努力，和多年来她为争取性别平权（gender equality）、为争取女性权益（fight for women）所做的努力。2016年9月21日，艾玛·沃特森现身联合国大会（UN General Assembly），为女性安全再次发声，代表"He For She（他为她）"运动发表消除校园暴力、保障女性安全的演讲。

Emma Watson: The Most Beautiful Girls Are Those Who Have Strong Heart

文◎ Emma Watson

Thank you all for being here for this important moment. These men from all over the world have decided to make gender equality a priority in their lives and in their universities. Thank you for making this commitment.

I graduated from university four years ago. I had always dreamed of going, and I know how fortunate I am to have had the opportunity to do so.

Brown became my home, my community, and I took the ideas and the experiences I had there into all of my social interactions, into my work place, into my politics, into all aspects of my life. I know that my university experience shaped who I am. And of course it does for many people.

But what if our experience in university shows us that women don't belong in leadership? What if it shows us that women can study, but they shouldn't lead a seminar? What if, as still in many places around the world, it tells us that women don't belong there at all? What if, as is the case in far too many universities, we are given the message that sexual violence isn't actually a form of violence?

But, we know that if you change students' experiences so that they have different expectations of the world around them, expectations of equality, society will change.

As we leave home for the first time to study at the places that we have worked so hard to get, we must not see or experience double standards. We need to see equal respect, leadership and pay.

The university experience must tell women that their brain power is valued, and not just that, but that they belong within the leadership of the university itself.

And so importantly right now, the experience must make it clear, that the safety of women, minorities, and anyone who may be vulnerable is a right, not a privilege.

A right that will be respected by a community that believes and supports survivors, and that recognizes that when one person's safety is violated, everyone feels their own safety is violated.

A university should be a place of refuge that takes

action against all forms of violence. That's why we believe that students should leave university believing in, striving for and expecting societies of true equality. Society of true equality in every sense. And universities have the power to be a vital catalyst for that change.

  Our ten impact champions have made this commitment and with their work, we know that they will inspire students, and other universities and schools across the world to do better.

  I am delighted to introduce this report on our progress, and I am eager to hear what's next.

  Thank you so much!

艾玛·沃特森：
内心强大的女性最美丽

文◎ Emma Watson（艾玛·沃特森）

非常感谢你们能在此见证这样一个重要的时刻。这些来自世界各地的人们已经决定把男女平等作为他们人生当中和大学校园里的一个重要议题。感谢你们的付出。

四年前，我大学毕业。我曾经一直梦想着自己可以去大学读书，并庆幸自己能有机会实现。

布朗大学成了我的家，我的归属。我把我在布朗大学里的想法和经历贯彻到我的社交、工作、政治以及生活的方方面面。我知道我在大学时期的经历塑造了今天的自己。当然，很多人都是如此。

但是，如果大学里的经历告诉我们女性不能成为领袖；告诉我们女性可以求学，但不能主持研讨会；告诉我们，就像世界上很多地区仍然表现的那样，女性根本不能上大学；像太多校园里的情况那样，让我们接受性暴力其实不属于暴力，我们该怎么办？

但是我们知道，如果大学改变了学生的经历，让他们对周遭的世界、对男女平等有了不同的期待，那么整个社会就将改变。

当我们第一次离开家去千辛万苦考取的学校求学时，我们不应当目睹和经历双重标准。我们应该看到同等的尊重、领导力和回报。

大学不仅要告诉女性她们的头脑是有价值的，还要告诉她们在大学里女性也可以成为领袖。

现如今同样重要的是，大学必须清楚地让学生知道：女性、少数族群和其他弱势群体的安全问题绝不是特权，而是他们的基本权利。

这种基本权利将被一个支持受害者并且相信若某一人的安全被侵犯，所有人都感同身受的社会所尊重。

大学应该是一个反对各种暴力行为的庇护所。这就是为什么我们认为一个离开大学的毕业生应该坚信且期待一个真正平等的社会，并为之努力奋斗。真正的平等应该体现在社会各个方面，大学有能力成为这种变革的重要加速器。

我们的十位影响力冠军为此做出了巨大贡献。通过他们的工作，我们知道他们将会激励学生和世界上其他的大学和学院做得更好。

我很高兴能够报告这些进展，也非常期待他们接下来的表现。非常感谢你们！

　　作为万千青少年的偶像，水果姐 Katy Perry（凯特·佩里）不仅带给大家许多好听的歌曲，更传递给众多粉丝满满的正能量。2013 年 5 月，Katy 就通过 Instagram（图片分享）给粉丝们写了下面这封极具正能量的信。一起来听听水果姐的金玉良言吧。

Be Proud of Who You Are

文◎ Katy Perry

　　That's right, folks. Be proud of who you are. Recently, I've been getting a lot of comments and tweets from fans who are struggling with self-harm or being a victim of bullying, Which brings tears to my eyes. I want you to be strong. There's only one you in this world, embrace it. And trust me, when you grow up and become successful, those bullies will wish they were friends with you and were nice to you.

Karma will do payback to them, just watch. When they bully again, just laugh in their faces or simply say I don't care. If they see it bothers you, they'll continue. If they see that you don't care and that it doesn't bother you, they'll stop! Simple! Stand up for yourself. Make those bullies look stupid. If it gets bad, you can simply tell the authority at school.

Another problem is a lot of kids these days who do self-harm. It's horrible to me. Don't ruin your skin. I think your skin is beautiful. Putting scars on your wrists or anywhere else is just heartbreaking for me. Cutting yourself doesn't fix anything. Just stop. For me, for you r family, for your friends, for you. I understand it's hard. I've never been through it but I have talked to fans like you. Just be clean for today, and see if you can go up to a week maybe? You can slowly progress to stop. I love you!

为自己骄傲

文◎ Katy Perry（凯特·佩里） 译◎ 赵越

是的，各位，为自己骄傲吧。最近我收到粉丝们的许多评论和推文，他们要么在纠结要不要自残，要么因成为被欺凌的对象而苦苦挣扎，这让我不禁落泪。我希望你们强大起来。这个世界

上只有一个你,欣然做自己吧。相信我,当你长大成人、功成名就之后,那些曾经欺负你的人就会希望自己曾和你做过朋友,希望自己当初友善待你。

因果报应会让他们付出代价的,等着瞧吧。等他们再欺负你的时候,当面嘲笑他们或者只说一句"我不在乎"就可以了。如果他们发现你很烦这个,他们就会继续欺负你。如果他们发现你并不在意,也没有被惹恼,他们就会收手!很简单!要为自己抗争,让那些恃强凌弱的人显得愚蠢无知。如果情况变得糟糕,你只需告诉学校里负责的老师就可以了。

还有一个问题是,如今有很多孩子会做出伤害自己的行为,这让我非常震惊。在我看来,你们的肌肤非常美丽,不要破坏它。你们在手腕或者身体的其他部位留下了疤痕,我会非常心痛的。伤害自己无济于事。为了我,也为了你们的亲朋好友,更为了你们自己,请停止这种行为。我知道这很难做到。虽然我没有经历过,但我与像你们这样有过自残行为的粉丝聊过天。首先尝试在今天之内不要伤害自己,再看看自己可不可以像这样坚持大概一个星期。你们会慢慢进步,直到最终不再做出伤害自己的事情。爱你们!

A Girl

文◎ Ezra Pound

The tree has entered my hands,
The sap has ascended my arms,
The tree has grown in my breast—
Downward,
The branches grow out of me, like arms.
Tree you are,
Moss you are,
You are violets with wind above them.
A child — so high — you are,
And all this is folly to the world.

少女

文◎庞德　译◎赵毅衡

树长进我的手心,
树叶升上我的手臂,
树在我的前胸,
朝下长,
树枝像手臂从我身上长出。
你是树,
你是青苔,
你是轻风吹拂的紫罗兰,
你是个孩子——这么高,
这一切对世人来说都是愚蠢的。

第二章

Madman's Diary
狂人日记

2

The Value of Time

文◎ Marilyn Monroe

To realize the value of one year:

Ask a student who has failed a final exam.

To realize the value of one month:

Ask a mother who has given birth to a premature baby.

To realize the value of one week:

Ask an editor of a weekly newspaper.

To realize the value of one hour:

Ask the lovers who are waiting to meet.

To realize the value of one minute:

Ask a person who has missed the train, bus or plane.

To realize the value of one second:

Ask a person who has survived an accident.

Time waits for no one.

Treasure every moment you have.

时间的价值

文◎凯瑟琳·桑

要想知道一年的价值:
就去问期末考试不及格的同学。
要想知道一个月的价值:
就去问生那早产儿的母亲。
要想知道一周的价值:
就去问问周报的编辑。
要想知道一小时的价值:
就去问等待相会的恋人。
要想知道一分钟的价值:
那就去问问误了火车汽车或飞机的人。
要想知道一秒的价值:
就去问大难不死的人。
时间不等人。
你拥有的每一分每一秒都要珍惜。

As Heroine of Every Mundane Day

文◎ Regena Thomashauer

I am the definition of a powerful woman.

I love with my whole body,

heart, and souls.

I say whatever is on my mind.

I rage with as much passion as I grieve.

I love my poetry,

my art.

I mother my child like a she-wolf.

I risk my life to live my truth.

I laugh easily,

mostly at myself.

I would see my soul for a night of ecstasy.

And every day I'm serving my goddess, and my god,

with every cell of my being.

In other words,

I am just like you.

平凡日子里的女英雄

译◎ Julie（朱莉）

我定义了"女强人"三个字。
我爱我的全部，
身心和灵魂。
我直言不讳。
我用力生气，
用力悲伤。
我爱我的诗歌，
我的艺术。
我像一匹母狼一样养育我的孩子。
我冒着生命危险真实地活着。
我轻松地大笑，
大多时候是笑自己。
我会在一个忘形的夜晚看见自己的灵魂。
每天我都全身心地为我的女神、我的上帝服务。
换句话说，
我和你一样。

Quotes of First Ladies: I Don't Want to Be a Saddle Horse

文◎ anonymous

电影 *Jackie*（《第一夫人》）是一部有关 Jacqueline Kennedy Onassis（杰奎琳·肯尼迪·奥纳西斯）或常常简称为 Jackie O 的传记片。第一夫人（the First Lady）通常指总统的妻子，其实也曾指代过总统的其他亲人，如女儿、侄女或儿媳。翻遍牛津出版的 *Oxford Essential Quotations*（《牛津必备引文词典》）一书，我们发现四条来自美国第一夫人的引文，在此与大家分享：

The one thing I do not want to be called is First Lady. It sounds like a saddle horse.

我不想被称为第一夫人，听起来像一匹驯马。

——*Jacqueline Kennedy Onassis*（杰奎琳·肯尼迪·奥纳西斯）

杰奎琳·肯尼迪·奥纳西斯是美国第 35 任总统约翰·肯尼迪的夫人。她没有绝世美貌，却是美国人心中最美的第一夫人，气质高贵、举止优雅、个性独立。她喜欢有挑战性的事物，很爱骑马。她曾经引领时尚潮流，冷静而又有些神秘。如以上引言所透露的，她并不甘于被称为第一夫人，不愿成为一匹驯马。

If you want to know the reason why I'm standing here, it's because of education. I never cut class.

如果你想知道我能站在这里的原因，那就是教育。我从不缺课。

——*Michelle Obama*（米歇尔·奥巴马）

这段话出自米歇尔·奥巴马 2009 年 4 月在英国伦敦伊斯灵顿的演讲。米歇尔·奥巴马是前任美国总统奥巴马的夫人，是美

我不愿成为一匹驯马
——那些美国第一夫人的名言

文◎佚名

国第一位非洲裔第一夫人。她也积极参加促进女性教育的诸多活动，其平民出身，以及从哈佛大学法学院博士生，到美国著名律师，到美国第一夫人的故事激励着很多女性。

A woman is like a teabag—only in hot water do you realize how strong she is.

女人就像茶包——只有在热水里你才发觉她有多厉害。

——*Nancy Reagan*（南希·里根）

这句话出自1981年3月29日《观察家报》的报道。南希·里根是美国第40任总统罗纳德·里根的妻子，是较有影响力的美国第一夫人。初任美国第一夫人时曾备受争议，但她几乎是用一生的时间去修炼，正如引言中所述，在滚烫的水里绽放。

Somewhere out in this audience may even be someone who will one day follow in my footsteps, and preside over the White House as the President's spouse. I wish him well!

在今天的听众中也许会有人接我的班，作为总统的配偶管理白宫，同时我也希望有人能成为总统。

——*Barbara Bush*（芭芭拉·布什）

出自芭芭拉·布什1990年在韦尔斯利学院（Wellesley College）的毕业演讲。芭芭拉·皮尔斯·布什为美国第41任总统乔治·布什的夫人，总统小布什和州长杰布·布什的母亲。在美国，人们都怀着崇敬的心情称她为贤妻良母，她把自己的一生默默地奉献给了她的亲人。这次演讲并不是很官方很空洞的演说，既没有热血沸腾，也不是慷慨激昂，更像是一位母亲以朴实亲切的言谈和轻松自然的幽默，向即将大学毕业的女儿述说过来人的经验。

乔布斯离开我们六年了。1997年，他回归苹果公司后，为了重新塑造苹果公司的精神内核，他亲自为广告片《非同凡响》撰写文本并配音。这支广告片帮助苹果公司走出破产的阴影，进而成为全球市值最高的公司，完成了自我救赎。

Think Different

文© anonymous

Here's to the crazy ones.

The misfits. The rebels. The troublemakers.

The round pegs in the square holes.

The ones who see things differently.

They're not fond of rules.

And they have no respect for the status quo.

You can quote them, disagree with them, glorify or vilify them.

About the only thing you can't do is to ignore them.

Because they change things.

They push the human race forward.

And while some may see them as the crazy ones, we see genius.

Because the people who are crazy enough to think they can change the world, are the ones who do.

非同凡响

文◎佚名

向那些疯狂的家伙致敬。
他们特立独行，他们桀骜不逊，他们惹是生非。
他们与世界格格不入。
他们用与众不同的眼光看待事物。
他们不喜欢墨守成规。
他们也不愿安于现状。
你可以引用他们，反对他们，颂扬或是诋毁他们。
但唯独不能漠视他们。
因为他们改变了世界。
他们推动人类向前发展。
一些人把他们视为疯子，但我们却视其为天才。
因为只有那些疯狂到以为自己能够改变世界的人，才能真正地改变世界。

第三章

YOLO 只活一次

Motto of Youth: YOLO

文◎ Yaning

YOLO is the abbreviation for: you only live once.

Similar to "carpe diem" or "memento mori", it implies that one should enjoy life, even if that entails taking risks.

It has become a popular Twitter hashtag. Some youth have said that it is their motto, and actor Zac Efron has a tattoo with the acronym. The phrase and acronym are used in merchandise worn by teenagers such as hats and t-shirts.

当下年轻人的座右铭——YOLO

文◎ Yaning（亚宁）

《牛津英语词典》被称为英语世界的金科玉律，已有150年历史，目前收录有80多万个词条，每3个月修订更新一次。在最近的这次更新中，被收录的部分新词其实早已广泛流传，比如YOLO。

YOLO 是 "you only live once"（你只活一次）首字母的缩略词。

YOLO 和"活在当下"或"死亡警告"类似，意思是人们应该享受生活，即使需要承担风险。

YOLO 已经成为推特上流行的话题标签。有些年轻人称YOLO 是自己的座右铭，演员扎克·埃夫隆还刺了一个该缩写的文身。这一缩写词还被用在青少年穿戴的帽子和T恤等商品上面。

I Am Not Pretty. I Am Not Beautiful. I Am as Radiant as the Sun

文◎ anonymous

Love myself I do. Not everything, but I love the good as well as the bad. I love my crazy lifestyle, and I love my hard discipline. I love my freedom of speech and the way my eyes get dark when I'm tired. I love that I have learned to trust people with my heart, even if it will get broken. I am proud of everything that I am and will become.

我不可爱，我也不漂亮，但我也能像太阳一样耀眼

文◎佚名

我爱自己。虽然对自己不是 100% 满意，但我在爱自己优点的同时，也爱我的缺点。我爱自己疯狂的生活方式，爱自己严格的自制力。我爱自己自由的言论，也爱因疲惫而暗沉的双眼。我爱自己用心去相信别人，即便最后可能会心碎。我为现在和未来的自己感到自豪。

《纽约时报》畅销书作家 Todd Parr（托德·帕尔）生长于怀俄明州，1995 年移居加州后开始追求自己的兴趣，展开艺术家的生涯，1998 年出版第一本著作，至今已创作三十多本童书绘本。Parr 喜爱画画涂鸦（尽管美术课曾经不及格）、喜爱动物、喜欢通心粉、喜欢起司，最爱两只宝贝狗：Pete 和 Tater Tot。绘画创作之外，Parr 也替芝麻街美语制作短片，及制作学龄前的电视节目 Todd World（《托德世界》），并以 Todd World 获艾美奖提名肯定。Todd Parr 的作品个人风格非常强烈，以粗黑的线条、鲜艳的色彩、简单的图案及文字呈现，借由作品传达爱的力量；要相信自我、善于助人，接受异同，世界因"你"而更美好。

It's Okay to Be Different

文◎ Todd Parr

It's okay to be missing a tooth (or two or three).

It's okay to need some help.

It's okay to have a different nose.

It's okay to be a different color.

It's okay to have no hair.

It's okay to have BIG ears.

It's okay to have wheels.

It's okay to be small, medium, large, extra large.

It's okay to wear glasses.

It's okay to talk about your feelings.

It's okay to eat macaroni and cheese in the bathtub.

It's okay to say NO to bad things.

It's okay to come from a different place.

It's okay to be embarrassed.

It's okay to come in last.

It's okay to dance by yourself.

It's okay to have a pet worm.

It's okay to be proud of yourself.

It's okay to have different Moms.

It's okay to have different Dads.

It's okay to be adopted.

It's okay to have an invisible friend.

It's okay to do something nice for someone.

It's okay to lose your mittens.

It's okay to get mad.

It's okay to do something nice for yourself.

It's okay to help a squirrel collect nuts.

It's okay to have different kinds of friends.

It's okay to make a wish.

It's okay to be different.

You are special and important.

Just because of being who you are.

不一样没关系

文◎ Todd Parr（托德·帕尔）

缺几颗牙没关系。
需要帮助没关系。
长了与众不同的鼻子也没关系。
肤色不同没关系。
没有头发没关系。
有一双大大的耳朵也没关系。
坐轮椅没关系。
身材瘦小，适中，胖，特胖都没关系。
戴眼镜也没关系。
说出你的感受没关系。
在浴缸里吃通心粉和奶酪没关系。
对不好的事情说"不"也没关系。
出身不同没关系。
感觉尴尬没关系。
得最后一名也没关系。
独自跳舞没关系。
养一只小虫子当宠物没关系。
为自己骄傲也没关系。

妈妈和别人的不一样没关系。
爸爸和别人的不一样没关系。
是一个被领养的小孩也没关系。
有一位看不见的朋友没关系。
为其他人做善事没关系。
弄丢你的连指手套也没关系。
生气没关系。
做点儿对自己好的事没关系。
帮一只松鼠收集坚果也没关系。
有各种各样的朋友没关系。
许个愿望没关系。
与众不同也没关系。
你是特别的，重要的。
因为你在做真实的自己。

It Is a Lot More Dangerous for a Plane to Stay on the Ground

文◎ anonymous

I learned a fact about airplanes the other day. This was—this was so surprising to see, I was talking to a pilot and he told me that many of his passengers think planes are dangerous to fly in. But he said actually, it is a lot more dangerous for a plane to stay on the ground. I say what? Like how does that sound what he said, he said because on the ground, the plane starts to rust.

Malfunction and wear, much faster than it ever would if it was in the air. As I walked away I thought, yeah, makes total sense because planes were built to live in the skies. And every person was built to live out the dream they have inside. So it is perhaps the saddest loss to live a life on the ground without ever taking off.

The television execs fired Oprah and said she was unfit for TV but she kept going. Critics told Beyoncé that she couldn't sing and she went through depression. But she kept going.

Struggle and criticisms are prerequisites for greatness. That is the law of this universe and no one escapes it. Because pain is life but you can choose what type? Either the pain on the road to success or the pain of being haunted with regret.

We have been given a gift that we call life. So don't blow it. You're not defined by your past, instead you were born anew in each moment. So own it now.

待在地上的飞机更危险

文◎佚名

讲一件我最近了解到的关于飞机的事实吧——实在出乎我意料。在我与一位飞行员聊天时他告诉我,很多乘客都认为飞机的状态在天上比地上危险,而事实上,待在地上的飞机更危险。我说:"什么,我没听错吧?"他解释道,飞机在地上会更快生锈。

飞机在地上产生磨损和故障的频率远远高于在天上飞的时候。后来我又想了想,对呀,很有道理,因为飞机是为翱翔天空而生,就像人是为活出本我探寻内心的梦而生。所以或许人生最应悲怜的是,在地上奋斗一辈子,却未曾起飞。

美国电视台的高管曾经开除过奥普拉(美国著名主持人)且说她不上镜,但她坚持了,依旧前行。碧昂斯(美国天后级歌手)曾被乐评人断言她不适合唱歌,她还曾因此患上了抑郁症,但是她坚持了,依旧前行。

抗争和承受批判是向卓越成就进发的先决条件。这是存于世间的法则,没有人能置身事外。因为痛苦是人生的一部分,但你可以选择它的方向,是通向成功的苦痛,还是抱憾终身的痛苦?

我们生而有一份珍贵的礼物,它叫人生。所以别糟蹋它。过去已成,但它无法定义现在,你永远活在现在,每一刻都是新生。所以,活在当下。绘英语

You are One of a Kind

文© anonymous

You may say that you don't have the imagination of J. K. Rowling. To create a world that can inspire millions of young people to read again at a time when everyone thought that only video games could attract them.

You may say that you don't have the creativity of Steve Jobs. To see the possibilities for individuals to have access to technology at their fingertips.

You may say that you don't have the vision of John F. Kennedy. To see the impossible as possible and to inspire an entire nation to get behind the effort.

You may say that you don't have the oratory skills of Martin Luther King. To put the need for change front and center on the agenda of his country and to move people to effect that change.

You do have the power to imagine a better world and make a difference in your own life and the life of others. Your imagination flows from your unique genetic make-up and your personal experiences.

No one else— who has ever walked on this earth, is here now, or ever will be— can duplicate what you have and who you are. You are one of a kind!

Just imagine! How will you leave the world a better place? What are you doing now to make a difference in the lives of others?

独一无二的你

文◎佚名

你也许会说,你没有 J. K. 罗琳那样的想象力,能创造一个魔法世界,激励千百万年轻人重拾书本阅读,而那个年代所有人都曾以为年轻人只会对电脑游戏感兴趣。

你也许会说,你没有史蒂夫·乔布斯那样的创造力,能预见到人们可以如此方便地使用高科技。

你也许会说,你没有约翰·F. 肯尼迪那样的远见卓识,视不可能为可能,并激励整个国家支持这项事业。

你也许会说,你没有马丁·路德·金那样的演讲才能,能把变革需求列入国家日程的优先考虑之列,能促使人们参与到变革中来。

但你的的确确有能力想象一个更美好的世界,给自己的生活以及他人的生活带来改变。你的想象力就来自你独特的基因组成和你的个人经历。

没有任何人——无论是这个星球上的古人、今人还是来者——能与你有同样的东西,能成为另一个你。你是独一无二的!

想想吧!你将如何令世界变得美好?现在你能做些什么改变他人的生活?

10 Things to Do Even if They Judge You

文◎ Marc

What would you do differently if you knew nobody would judge you?

Truth be told, no one has the right to judge you. People may have heard your stories, but they can't feel what you are going through; they aren't living your life. So forget what they say about you. Focus on how you feel about yourself, and do what you know in your heart is right.

Here are ten things to do even if others judge you for it:

1. Take care of yourself. Your relationship with yourself is the closest and most important relationship you will ever have. If you don't take good care of yourself, then you can't take good care of others either; which is why taking care of yourself is the best selfish thing you can do. Read *The Mastery of Love*.

2. Do what you know is right, for you.—Don't be scared to walk alone, and don't be scared to like it. Don't let anyone's ignorance, drama, or negativity stop you from being the best you can be. Keep doing what you know in your heart is right, for you. Because when you are totally at peace within yourself, nothing can shake you.

3. Follow your own unique path. Every new day is a chance to change your life. Work on making life all that you want it to be. Work hard for what you believe, and keep your dreams big and your worries small. You never need to

carry more than you can hold; just take it one day at a time. And while you're out there making decisions instead of excuses, learning new things, and getting closer and closer to your goals, know that there are others out there, like me, who admire your efforts and are striving for greatness too.

4. Lock yourself away from the world and work on your goals. Dream big dreams, but realize that short term, realistic goals are the key to success. Success is directly connected with daily action. The way we spend our time defines who we are. Successful people keep moving, by doing small things every day that bring them a couple steps closer to their dream. They make mistakes along the way, but they don't quit — they learn and press on. Read *Getting Things Done*.

5. Adjust your goals and dreams as life changes. A great deal of pain in life comes from having a specific dream that you've fallen in love with, and when it doesn't work out exactly as planned, you become angry that you now have to pursue a different path. If you want to tame your inner demons and make the most of life, you must not become rigidly attached to just one specific dream, and remain open to there being an even better, equally as happy path

ahead. Life is unpredictable, but it provides plenty of opportunities to make dreams come true. Just don't forget that sometimes taking a positive step forward requires you to slightly adjust your dreams, or plan new ones — it's OK to change your mind or have more than one dream.

6. Forgive those who have wronged you. Forgiveness is a gift you give yourself. Forgiveness is an attribute of the strong and wise. Forgiveness allows you to focus on the future without combating the past. To understand the potential of everything going forward is to forgive everything already behind you. Without forgiveness, wounds can never be healed, and moving on can never be accomplished. What happened in the past is just one chapter. Don't close the book, just turn the page.

7. Show everyone your love and kindness. If you are reserving your love only for those who you have decided are worthy of it — all strangers excluded — it may come as a surprise to learn that this is not love at all, it is called judgment. Judgment is selective, love is all embracing. Just as the sunlight and the wind do not discriminate, true love does not make any such distinctions either. Love and kindness is a way of living. Where there is love, there is no judgment. Where there is judgment, there is no love. Read

The 5 Love Languages.

8. Stand up for others, even if it's the unpopular thing to do. Sometimes you will say something really small and simple, but it will fit right into an empty space in someone's heart. Dare to reach into the darkness, to pull someone else into the light. Remember, strong people stand up for themselves, but stronger people stand up for others too, and lend a hand when they're able.

9. Fight through your failures. When you are feeling down or dealing with failure, don't be ashamed. There's nothing to be ashamed of. You are going through a difficult time, and you are still pushing forward. That's something to be proud of — that you are fighting through it and slowly rising above it. Let everyone know that today you are a lot stronger than you were yesterday, and you will be.

10. Keep your head held high and keep on smiling. Every day of your life is a page of your history. The only time you run out of chances is when you stop taking them. Don't cry over the past, cry to get over the past. Don't smile to hide the pain, smile to heal the pain. Don't think of all the sadness in the world, think of all the beauty that still remains around you.

即使别人评头论足，也要去做的10件事

文◎ Marc（马克）

如果你知道没人会对你评头论足，做法是否会不一样呢？

说真的，没人有权利对你说三道四。人们可能听说过你的事情，但他们并没有切身体会；他们又没过着你的生活。所以别理会他人说什么。专注自己的感受，并且去做你内心认为是正确的事情。

即使别人评头论足，你也一定要去做以下十件事情：

1. 照顾好自己。——在所有的关系中，每个人和自我的关系是最紧密的，也是最重要的。如果你不能照顾好自己，那么也就无法照顾好别人。所以，各种自私行为中，照顾好自己是最好的一桩事情。读读《掌握爱》这本书吧。

2. 为自己，做你认为正确的事情。——别害怕孤身上路；而且，如果喜欢独自行走，也不要觉得这个念头可怕。别让旁人的无知愚昧、大惊小怪或者消极态度阻挡了你的脚步，让你不能做最好的自己。内心认定正确的事情，就坚持去做，只为你自己。因为，当你和自我处于完全和谐的状态时，就没人可以动摇你了。

3. 走自己独特的道路。——每天都是改变生活的机会。努力经营，往渴望的生活方向前进。为自己相信的事情，艰苦奋斗；心怀远大，藐视忧虑。量力而行，不用超负荷；只要每天都有进步。还有，在没有做之前，你要决定是否去做，而不是找借口，并且要学习新知识，越来越接近自己的目标；你会知道还有些旁人，

像我一样，佩服你的努力，而且，我们都是追求卓越的同路人。

4.远离喧嚣，努力向着目标前进。——梦想需远大，但要知道短期的、现实可行的目标才是成功的关键。成功与日常行为直接相关。如何支配时间决定了我们是怎样的人。日常的点点滴滴，日积月累，逐渐向着梦想靠拢，成功人士通过这么做，一直保持前进。一路上，他们也会犯错，但他们不放弃——他们吸取教训，坚持下来。读读《去做事》这本书吧。

5.当生活改变时，调整目标和梦想。——人生很多不如意来自你真心喜爱某一梦想，但事与愿违，于是人变得怨天尤人了，这个时候，你得寻找另外一条路了。如果要想驯服心中的恶魔，并且发挥生命的最大价值，那么，千万别执迷于某一特定的梦想；当前方有一条更好的、让人同样幸福的道路时，要保持开放的心态。生活无常，但它还是给实现梦想提供了很多机会。只是别忘记：有时候，迈出积极的一步，需要你略微调整梦想，或者筹划新的梦想——改主意或者有了更多的梦想，这些都是正常的。

6.原谅那些不曾善待你的人。——原谅别人是你送给自己的一份礼物。坚强和明智的人才有资格去原谅。原谅让你将注意力集中到未来，而不是与往事纠缠。原谅所有的往事，才能理解未来的潜力。没有原谅，伤口永远无法愈合，那么就无法前进。无论过去发生过什么，都只是人生的章节。不要合上书，只要翻过

那一页。

7.给予别人爱心和善意。——爱心如果只给那些你认为值得的人,而排除了所有的陌生人,那么这就不是爱心,这叫私心。得出这样的结论,或许会令人意外吧。私心挑三拣四,爱心拥抱一切。就像阳光和风对众生一视同仁,真正的爱心也应如此不偏不倚。爱心和善意是一种生活方式。有爱心的地方,私心消弭无踪。私心出没的地方,爱心无处藏身。读读《五种爱的语言》这本书吧。

8.即使不招人待见,也要支持他人。——有时候,你只说了只言片语,却能触动别人空洞的心灵。鼓起勇气去触摸黑暗吧,将他人拉进阳光里。记住,强大的人坚持自我;但更强大的人也会为别人挺身而出,当有能力的时候,他们会对别人施以援手。

9.从失败中,杀出一条路来。——当觉得走下坡路了,或者面临失败,不要觉得羞愧。没什么好羞愧的。你正处在艰难时期,但还要继续前进。你一路杀将过来,慢慢有了起色,这就是值得骄傲的事情。让每个人都知道:今天的你比昨天的你更加强大,而未来的你又强过今天的你。

10. 要一直抬起头,并且保持笑容。——生命的每一天都是人生道路上的一页篇章。除非生命停止,否则永远都有机会。不要为过去哭泣,而是祈祷能跨过昨日的那道坎儿。不要强颜欢笑去隐藏伤痛,要带着笑意去治愈伤口。不要老想着人世间的哀伤愁苦,要想想那些依然围绕着你的诸般美好。 绘英语

You Should Become a Conduit of Light

文◎ Emily Madill

When you love who you are,
you become a conduit of light.
Just drop into your heart space,
and live life from this view.
For all of this doing
is not who you are.
Listen to your heart's soft whisper,
this voice will show you the way.
Live life from your essence
is what she will say.
See the light in yourself,
and your world will be bright.
There is no need to worry,
you are exactly as you should be;
remember to love who you are,
and love you will see.

你要成为自己的那道光

文◎ Emily Madill（艾米丽·马歇尔）

当你爱自己的时候，
你会成为一道光。
只需触及心房，
并遵循本心来生活。
做这一切
无关你是谁。
聆听内心轻柔的呢喃，
她会告诉你方法。
遵循本性来生活
她会这样告诉你。
欣赏自身的光芒，
你的世界都会变得明亮。
没必要担心，
你正是自己本来的模样；
记得爱自己，
爱自己欣赏的一切。

Are You That Elephant Stuck Right Where You Were

文◎ anonymous

As a man was passing the elephants, he suddenly stopped, confused by the fact that these huge creatures were being held by only a small rope tied to their front leg. No chains, no cages. It was obvious that the elephants could, at anytime, break away from their bonds but for some reason, they did not.

He saw a trainer nearby and asked why these animals just stood there and made no attempt to get away. "Well," trainer said, "when they are very young and much smaller we use the same size rope to tie them and, at that age, it's enough to hold them. As they grow up, they are conditioned to believe they cannot break away. They believe the rope can still hold them, so they never try to break free."

The man was amazed. These animals could at any time break free from their bonds but because they believed they couldn't, they were stuck right where they were.

Like the elephants, how many of us go through life hanging onto a belief that we cannot do something, simply because we failed at it once before?

你也是那头被困住的大象吗

文◎佚名

当一名男子经过象群的时候,他突然停了下来。这群庞大生物被一根系在它们前腿的小绳子拴住了,他对此十分困惑。没有锁链,没有笼子。显然,任何时候大象们都可以挣脱束缚,然而,由于某种原因,它们并没有挣脱。

他看到附近的训练员,问道,为什么这些动物只是站在那儿,却不尝试逃脱。"嗯!"训练员说,"在它们很小的时候,我们用同样尺寸的绳子拴着它们,那个时候,这条绳子足够拴住它们了。随着它们渐渐长大,它们习惯性地认为自己无法挣脱。它们以为这条绳子依然可以束缚住自己,所以它们从不会尝试挣脱。"

这名男子十分惊讶。这些动物本来随时都可以挣脱束缚,然而因为它们认为自己无法挣脱,所以它们就被困在了那里。

就像这些大象,我们之中有多少人在生活中固守着一个观念,自己办不到某件事情,只是因为曾经失败过一次?

Circle

文◎ Zhang Zhizhong

When I was a child,
I liked making circles aground with a mothball,
To encircle the ants within.
When I am grown up,
I wonder who has made a circle for me,
And I cannot but move about within.

圈

文◎张智中

小时候,
我用卫生球在地上画圈,
把蚂蚁圈在里面。
长大后,
是谁给我画了一个圈,
让我一辈子都在里面转。

Don't Be What They Make You

文◎ Hugh Jackman

　　In seventeen years I've changed a lot. In my life someone described me as stubborn Hugh.

　　It is not easy to change direction. It is hard to convince everyone. It is hard to get everyone on board. But I have a small group.

　　I've learn a lot from this character, to be true to yourself. When Logan says "don't be what they make you", it is a powerful line I think it relates to everybody.

　　It's calling to do something unique to us, to be ourselves. Be respectful, look after people we loved but always stay true to yourself. And I think I've learned this from this character.

别按"他们"的期待
过你自己的人生

文◎休·杰克曼

这 17 年我改变了很多。曾经有人叫我"固执休"。

改变一件事的走向很难。因为去说服所有人很难，召唤他们和你共同做一件事更难，好在慢慢我们有了一个固定的团队。

我从（金刚狼）这个角色中学到，要忠于自己。罗根说："不要按照'他们'的期待过你自己的人生。"这句台词充满力量，而且适用于我们每个人。

这句话就像一个召唤一样，鼓励你去做与众不同的事情，去做真正的自己。我们要对身边的人给予尊重，要关心照顾你所爱的人，但要永远忠于自己。我觉得这是我从这个角色身上学到的最重要的东西。绘英语

You Have to Be You, Before You Can Be Them

文◎ anonymous

You want to be like the famous actor, Brad Pitt.

You want to be like the talented basketball player, Lebron James.

You want to be like the brilliant innovator, Bill Gates.

Listen to me: You can't get to that level. You can't get to that level until you start to invest in your mind.

You've spent so much time with other people. You've spent so much time trying to get people to like you, you know other people more than you know yourself! And you know what? You've invested so mush time in them, you don't even know who you are!

I challenge you to spend time by yourself.

But for people who are chasing their dreams, life has a special sort of meaning. When you become the "right person", what you do is you start separating yourself from other people. You begin to have a certain uniqueness. As long as you follow other people, as long as you're being a copy-cat, you will never ever be the best copy-cat in the world.

I challenge you to define your value.

Not everyone will see it. Not everyone will join you. Not everyone will have the vision. It's necessary to know that. You are an uncommon breed! It's necessary that you align yourself with people and attract people into your business . People who are unstoppable and unreasonable. People who refuse to leave life just as it is and who want more!

I challenge you to invest in you.

Someone's opinion of you does not have to become your reality. You don't have to go through life being a victim. And even though you face disappointments, you must know within yourself, that you can do this. Even if no one helps you see to it, you must see it for yourself.

Don't let anybody steal your dream. You may fail, and fail, and fail again. But you're, reviewing it everyday and saying to yourself...

"It's not over until I win."

You can live your dream.

在成为他们之前，
请先成为你自己

译◎ Julie（朱莉）

你希望成为像布拉德·皮特那样知名的演员。
你希望成为像勒布朗·詹姆斯那样的天才篮球运动员。
你希望成为像比尔·盖茨那样杰出的创新者。
听我一句吧：你到不了那样的高度，除非你开始修炼自己的内心。

你浪费了太多时间在别人身上，浪费了太多时间让别人来喜欢你，你对别人的了解甚至比自己还要多！可是你知道吗？你花了太多精力在他们身上，甚至不知道自己是谁了。

我向你发出挑战：学会独处。

但对追逐梦想的人来说，人生有一种特殊的意义。当你成为那个"对的人"，你就会把自己从别人身上剥离。你开始拥有独一无二的特质。一旦你追随他人的脚步，一旦你成了别人的模仿者，你就永远不会成为最棒的模仿者。

我向你发出挑战：衡量自己的价值。

并不是所有人都会看清你的价值，不是所有人会和你一样，有那样的眼光。知道这一点很重要。也许在他们眼里，你就是个怪人！你必须和那些富有激情的人交友，吸引他们加入你的行列。那些人势不可当，甚至有些不可理喻，他们不愿苟且度日，渴望更精彩的人生！

我向你发出挑战：修炼自己。

别人对你的评价不一定就会成真，你也不必成为这些言语的受害者。即使面对失败，你内心深处也要明白，自己可以做到。即使没有人帮助你搞明白这一点，也必须相信自己。

不要让任何人偷走你的梦想。你也许会一次又一次跌倒，但你仍然要反复对自己说……

"还没有胜利，这就不算结局。"

你能够成就自己的梦想。

Each One of Us Is Alone in the World

文© Maugham

Each one of us is alone in the world. He is shut in a tower of brass, and can communicate with his fellows only by signs, and the signs have no common value, so that their sense is vague and uncertain. We seek pitifully to convey to others the treasures of our heart, but they have not the power to accept them, and so we go lonely, side by side but not together, unable to know our fellows and unknown by them. We are like people living in a country whose language they know so little that, with all manner of beautiful and profound things to say, they are condemned to the banalities of the conversation manual. Their brain is seething with ideas, and they can only tell you that the umbrella of the gardener's aunt is in the house.

我们生来就是孤独的
——《月亮与六便士》

文◎ Maugham（毛姆）

我们每个人生在世界上都是孤独的。每个人都被囚禁在一座铁塔里，只能依靠一些符号同别人传达自己的思想。而这些符号并没有共同价值，因此它们的意义是模糊的、不确定的。我们非常可怜地想把自己心中的财富传送给别人，但是他们却没有接受这些财富的能力。因此我们只能孤独地行走，尽管身体互相依傍却并不在一起，既不了解别人，也不能被别人了解。我们好像住在异国的人，对于这个国家的语言懂得非常少，虽然我们有各种美妙的深奥的事情要说，却只能局限于会话手册上的那几句陈腐、平庸的话。我们的脑子里充满了各种思想，而我们能说的只不过是像"园丁的姑母有一把伞在屋子里"这类话。绘英语

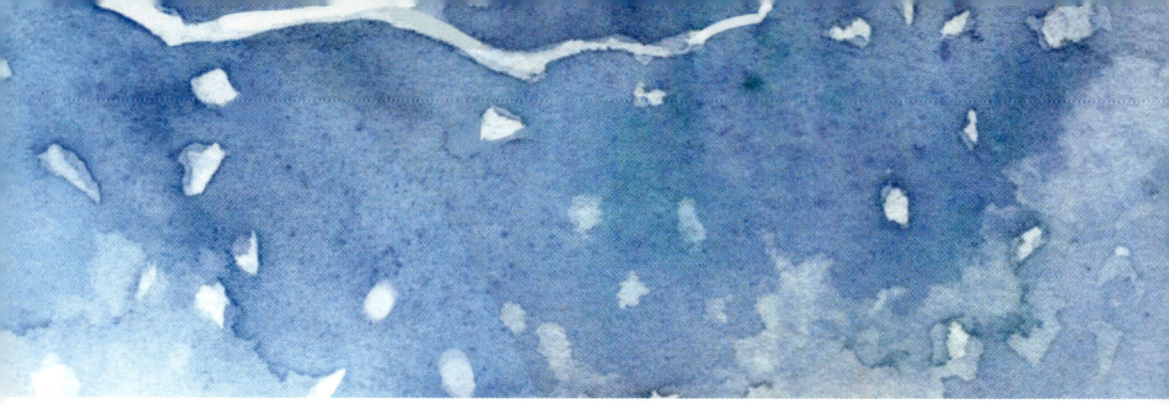

The Life I Desired

文◎ Maugham

That must be the story of innumerable couples, and the pattern of life it offers has a homely grace. It reminds you of a placid rivulet, meandering smoothly through green pastures and shaded by pleasant trees, till at last it falls into the vastly sea; but the sea is so calm, so silent, so indifferent, that you are troubled suddenly by a vague uneasiness. Perhaps it is only by a kink in my nature, strong in me even in those days, that I felt in such an existence, the share of the great majority, something amiss. I recognized its social value. I saw its ordered happiness, but a fever in my blood asked for a wilder course. There seemed to me something alarming in such easy delights. In my heart was desire to live more dangerously. I was not unprepared for jagged rocks and treacherous, shoals it I could only have change—change and the excitement of unforeseen.

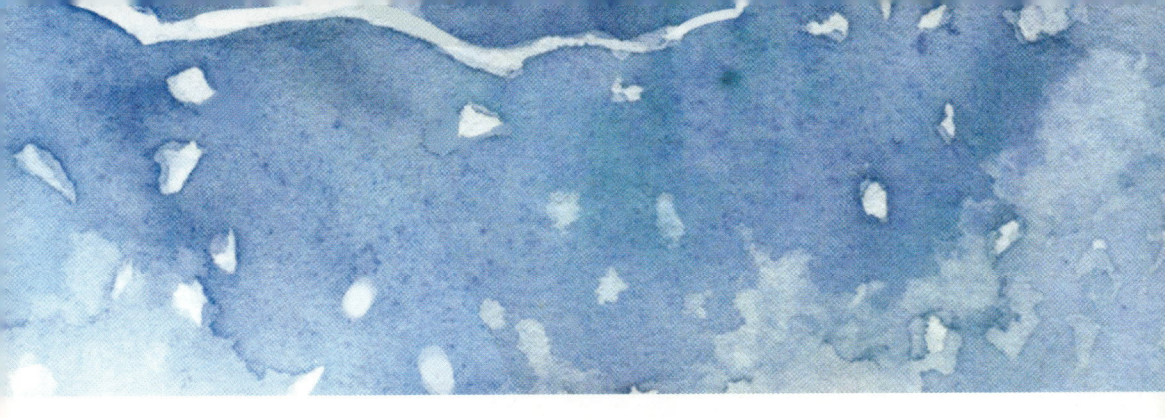

我所追求的生活

文◎ Maugham（毛姆）

　　这一定是世间无数对夫妻的生活写照，这种生活模式给人一种天伦之美。它使人想起一条平静的溪流，蜿蜒畅游过绿茵的草场，浓荫遮蔽，最后注入烟波浩渺的汪洋大海。但是大海太过平静，太过沉默，太过不动声色，你会突然感到莫名的不安。也许这只是我自己的一种怪诞想法，在那样的时代，这想法对我影响很深：我觉得这像大多数人一样的生活，似乎欠缺了一点儿什么。我承认这种生活有社会价值，我也看到了它那井然有序的幸福，但我血液里的冲动却渴望一种更桀骜不驯的旅程。这样的安逸中好像有一种叫我惊惧不安的东西。我的心渴望一种更加惊险的生活。只要生活中还能有变迁——以及不可知的刺激，我愿意踏上怪石嶙峋的山崖，奔赴暗礁满布的海滩。绘英语

《月光男孩》在第89届奥斯卡奖中获得8项提名,最终夺得小金人。本片改编自舞台剧《月光下,黑色男孩看来好似蓝色》,剧名充满诗意。男孩奇伦成长过程中所遇到的每个问题,在学校遭受霸凌,对自我的探索,疑惑与恐惧,对你我都并不陌生,也或多或少是我们成长故事中的一段。本文节选自该片的台词。你怎么定义自己,你就会成为什么样的人。

Moonlight: At Some Point, You Gotta Decide for Yourself Who You're Going to Be

文 © anonymous

1. At some point, you gotta decide for yourself who you're going to be. Can't let nobody make that decision for you.

2. I wasn't never really worth shit. Never really did anything I actually wanted to do. All I could do was to do what folks thought I should be doing.

3. It just come through the hood and it's like everything stop for a second. Because everyone just wanna feel it. Everything just get quiet. And it's like you can hear is your own heartbeat.

4. I cry so much sometimes. I feel like I'm gon' just turn into drops. Think you can roll out into the water, roll out into the water.

5. Lord knows I did not have love for you when you needed it.

6. It's all love and pride in this house.

7. In moonlight...black boys look blue.

8. You're the only one.

《月光男孩》：
总有一天，你要自己决定成为什么样的人

文◎佚名

1. 总有一天，你要自己决定成为什么样的人，别让其他人替你做主。

2. 我一直一无是处，基本没做过真正想做的事。我能做的也就是干一些别人觉得我该干的事。

3. 风从你的头顶缓缓吹过，那一刻感觉就像是时间静止了，因为你只想一心一意地感受它。周围的一切都将变得安静。你所能听到的只有自己的心跳声。

4. 我经常哭，因为有时我感觉自己渺小得就像是一个水滴，觉得自己会坠入那片汪洋中，被大海吞噬。

5. 上帝知道我没有在你需要的时候给你我的爱。

6. 这里只有爱和骄傲。

7. 月光下的黑人男孩是蓝色的。

8. 你是唯一。 绘英语

第四章

Freckle Girl
雀斑少女

How the First Ladies Take the Fashion Lead

文◎ Sarah Young

First ladies of the United States have not only had a major influence on the course of the country throughout the years, but have also stood at the forefront of fashion. Here, we take a look at how these women embraced the role clothes can play in establishing substance.

Michelle Obama

Not since Jackie Kennedy has the US had such a fashionable leading lady. Michelle Obama's timeless style appealed to all generations while her affinity with high-low fashion choices made her feel just like 'one of us'. From everyday off-the-rack clothes to costume creations from some seriously heavy hitting designers like Jason Wu and Tom Ford, Michelle had a winning fashion formula. She has

taken some risks during her time as First Lady but never lost sight of her polished look, especially that trademark sleeveless fare.

Laura Bush

Having admitted that it was hard for her to be in the eye of the fashion critics, Laura Bush was never one to keep up with the trends, instead opting for a style categorised by harmless elegance rather than cutting edge fashion. For her first Inaugural Ball she wore a dress designed by a local designer from her homestate of Texas. Laura was the ultimate in classic, conservative style albeit with a punch of patriotic pride.

Hillary Clinton

Hillary has been dressing for the White House for decades now and in the process has seemingly carved herself adistinctive look; one which used to be defined by pastel two pieces and a no-nonsense bob with wispy bangs. Since then though her style has shifted and been repackaged with

the help of Obama's former aide Kristina Schake. Ultimately, her sartorial choices can be summarised in a single word — pantsuits.

Nancy Reagan

Former movie Star Nancy brought her fierce red carpet style to the White House as she ushered in a new era of Hollywood glamour. She regularly opted for striking "Reagan Red" and gold lamé over stale neutrals to really express her patriotism.

Jackie Kennedy

It might have been more than 20 years since her passing, but Jackie Kennedy is still a fashion role model for women all over the world. Best known for her ladylike pillbox hats and skirt suits, she chose pale colours that would look good in black-and-white and wasn't afraid to take risks in preppy cropped pants.

Betty Ford

She might not have been particularly trend setting but Betty certainly had style and a knack for fashion. With her signature 70s-style bob, silk scarves, cat-eye specs and high-neck Chinese-style collars, this First Lady oozed individual style in the best way possible.

历任美国第一夫人是如何引领时尚潮流的

文◎ Sarah Young（莎拉·杨）

历年来，美国的第一夫人们不仅在很大程度上影响着国家的进程，而且始终站在时尚的前沿。今天，我们就来看一看这些女人是如何通过服装来塑造个人形象的。

米歇尔·奥巴马

自杰奎琳·肯尼迪离开后，美国还没有出现过像米歇尔这么时尚的第一夫人。米歇尔·奥巴马的穿衣风格永不过时，受到了每一代人的欢迎。她平和亲民，又喜欢选择高质量、低价格的时装，让人感觉她就像"我们中的一员"。从适合日常穿着的平价成衣，到吴季刚、汤姆·福特等重量级设计师定制的精美华服，米歇尔已经成功打造出自己骄人的穿衣风格。在就任第一夫人期间，她也有几回差点儿"出漏子"，但她总是能让自己光彩照人，尤其是穿着标志性的无袖连衣裙时。

劳拉·布什

劳拉曾亲口承认自己很难得到时尚评论人士的青睐，她从不追求时髦，不穿前卫服装，却喜欢选择稳妥的优雅风格。在她的首场就职舞会上，劳拉穿了一件由家乡得克萨斯州的本土设计师设计的裙子。尽管劳拉是一位充满爱国自豪感的第一夫人，但她的穿衣风格极为经典保守。

希拉里·克林顿

迄今为止，希拉里已为白宫穿衣打扮数十载。在这个过程中，她好像塑造出了自己的独特风格。从前是浅色两件套加端庄短发配细碎刘海，后来曾改变过风格，也曾在奥巴马前任助理斯蒂娜·斯卡克的帮助下重新包装过，最后，她的着装选择可概括为一个词——裤装。

南希·里根

前影星南希将走红毯的大胆风格带进了白宫，就此引领白宫进入了好莱坞魅力新纪元。她平常更倾向于选择鲜艳夺目的"里根红"和炫亮金，而非没有生机的素净色，很好地展现了她的爱国情怀。

杰奎琳·肯尼迪

杰奎琳已逝世 20 多年了，但时至今日她依然是全球女性的时尚典范。最有名的是她那些尽显女士贤淑风范的小礼帽和西装裙。她喜欢选择浅色衣服，因为在当时的黑白电视上会更好看，杰奎琳还毫不畏惧穿上私校风格的短裤。

贝蒂·福特

贝蒂可能不是特别时髦，但她绝对穿出了自己的风格，在时尚方面很有自己的一套。标志性的 20 世纪 70 年代波波头、丝巾、猫眼眼镜、中式高领，这位第一夫人淋漓尽致地展现出了自己的个人风格。绘英语

Homely Looking People Will Not Easily Go Die

文◎ anonymous

When I was seven years old, I would put my school book bag on both my shoulders and had it sit plumb in the middle of my back, as backpacks were made to do.

One morning, when it was so frigid outside you could barely muster getting out of bed, my older brother joined me at the bus stop, and told me I was wearing my backpack wrong. He grabbed it, tossed it over my right shoulder with both straps on the same side and said, "There, that's better."

Then he said, "You're not pretty, so you have to try harder. OK?"

I stayed smiling because even at a young age, I understood the importance of pretending to not have emotions. In my household, it was a matter of survival. But what he said crushed me.

Soon thereafter, I started picking up on the signs one receives when they aren't attractive.

Mostly, I paid for not being conventionally attractive by being ignored or not included in "moments"—the many moments attractive people experience.

Many times, I walked into a room with all of my friends and witnessed them receiving compliments—everyone except me.

It took me being observant and honest to see I didn't belong. It took studying the aesthetics in photos taken by my friends and knowing something wasn't quite right. It's a lack of pride you know would be there if you were just prettier, or sexier. It's that you simply know that no matter what you do, sans literal plastic surgery, you will never belong to a certain club.

But here is where I throw you a curve ball: my being unattractive hasn't stopped me from living the other side's life.

I decided I would shoot out of my league. I made friends and dated people I shouldn't be allowed to date. I stepped over the line. I surrounded myself with individuals who are more educated, prettier or smarter than me, even in the face of people saying, quite literally, "they are out of your league."

I may not technically be the smartest or most beautiful person, but I run with those who are. I become by association, even a touch of such, even at a lower rank—beautiful. I buck the system.

To do so, yes, means you may be painfully aware of what you are and will never be. You will be defined by

what you have the nerve to aim at being. In doing so, you will challenge and question what smart is. You will not be generic, or predictable. Attractive is only what we define it to be. Don't pigeonhole yourself so quickly. Live the life you want to live—even if you didn't win the genetic lottery.

没有颜值的人不会轻易投降

文◎佚名

在我七岁那年，我会用双肩背书包，让它处在我背部的正中央，感觉双肩包就应该这么背。

某天早晨，外面寒风萧瑟，冷到你根本不想起床，我的哥哥跟我一同在车站等车，他告诉我我的双肩包背错了。他一把抓过来，将书包和两侧的背带甩至我的右肩，然后说："看，这就好多了。"

然后他说："你不漂亮，所以你要更加努力，明白吗？"

我的笑容凝固了，因为即便在青少年时期，我也知道假装不露声色的重要性。在我家里，这是一种生存技能。但是他说的让我感到崩溃。

此后，我开始关注人们对于低颜值人的反应。

很多时候，我因为没有高颜值而被人忽略或无法经历"某些时刻"——那些具有高颜值的人所经历的时刻。

  不知多少次我和朋友一起走进教室，然后看着她们接受别人的赞美，除了我之外每个人都有。

  我善于察言观色，而且很诚实，所以我知道我注定不合主流。我仔细研究我朋友照片中的美学，然后发现某些东西并非是真理。如果你仅仅是姿色更上一层楼，却缺乏油然而生的自豪感。你明白无论你怎样改变，除非整形，你永远不会属于高颜值的团体。

  但是现在我给你一剂药方：我不出众的相貌并不能阻止我拥有自己的生活。

  我决定扩展我的圈子，我和以前觉得不能交朋友的人交朋友，和以前觉得不能约的人约会。我越过了那条线，周围全是比我更有学识、更漂亮的人，甚至人们告诉我，非常实事求是地说"他们可不是你圈子里的人啊"。

  我也许不会是最聪明、最漂亮的人，但是我和这些人一同奋斗，哪怕仅有一点点提升，哪怕仍然没那么漂亮，我改变了这个固有的规则。

  是的，这样做你也许会痛苦地发现自己的真相，并再也不可能成为"漂亮"的人。你前进的目标将定义你自己。如此一来，你会挑战和质疑"聪慧"。你将成为个例或非等闲之辈。美丽仅仅是我们给的定义。别那么快地给自己归类，即使你没有天赋，也要活出自己的精彩。绘英语

Is It True that Imperfection Is the real Fashion?
Western Girls Are Crazy about Freckles Tattoos

文© anonymous

While some women cover their faces with thick layers of foundation to cover up natural freckles, others are apparently getting them tattooed. Yup, freckles are in, and some people would even go under the needle to get them.

Freckle tattooing is reportedly one of the fastest growing beauty treatments available today. Similar to microblading, an eyebrow enhancing procedure, freckle tattooing involves the use of pigments to ink freckle—like dots onto a person's face that eventually blend in with the client's skin tone. As with any tattoo, there is some inevitable swelling, but it subsides after a few months, and the initial dark coloring of the freckles fades to a light brown.

It's unclear when exactly freckle tattooing started, but Montreal-based cosmetic tattoo artist Gabrielle Rainbow is considered one of the pioneers who spearheaded the beauty trend. She says she was inspired by a friend who had become tired of constantly having to paint them on her face with makeup. Rainbow first experimented on herself, although she doesn't recommend tattooing your own face, and after seeing that the effect was very realistic, she decided to tattoo her friend as well.

Gabrielle Rainbow told *New Beauty* that she now tattoos face freckles for a wide range of clients, from people who naturally get them in the summertime who also want to keep them when they can't get enough sun exposure, to those who are freckle free, but always dreamed of sporting their own "sun kisses".

"In terms of the freckles, when they are 'freshly done,' they will appear swollen almost like bee stings, and the swelling will go down within a couple hours and you'll be left with your cute, fresh freckles," the cosmetic tattoo artist says. "Over the course of one to two months, the color will soften dramatically and look more natural. They will fade naturally with time, and if you wish to keep them you can always get the color boosted whenever you like."

Gabrielle Rainbow says she normally takes the "less is more" approach when it comes to freckles, but most of her clients love the result so much that the usually ask for more. However, the artist points out that people interested in having their faces tattooed need to do their research before going under the needle. With so much demand for the procedure these days, there are plenty of people looking to take advantage of naive clients, so Rainbow recommends finding artists who aren't afraid to show their portfolio and healed work.

"Even if this is 'semipermanent,' there are risks, such as technicians who will go too deep or not use the proper inks." the tattoo artist said.

原来不完美才是真流行?
欧美少女都在迷雀斑刺青

文◎佚名

有些女性会用厚厚的粉底来遮盖脸上天生的雀斑，而其他一些女性却要往自己的脸上文雀斑。雀斑如此流行，有人宁愿挨针扎也要让自己的脸上有雀斑。

据报道，雀斑刺青是如今发展最迅速的美容治疗项目之一。和微创提眉手术类似，雀斑刺青就是用染料将雀斑状的小点文到一个人的脸上，这些小斑点最终会和客户的肤色融为一体。和其他刺青一样，创伤处的红肿是不可避免的，但几个月后就会消退，最初文的深黑色也会渐渐变成浅褐色。

不知道雀斑刺青是什么时候兴起的，但是现在居住在加拿大蒙特利尔的美容文身技师加布里埃尔·雷恩博被认为是引领这一美容潮流的先驱之一。她表示，她是受一位疲于化雀斑妆的朋友的启发。雷恩博先在自己脸上做了试验，尽管她不推荐在脸上做刺青，但是看到效果很逼真，她决定在她朋友脸上也文上雀斑。

加布里埃尔·雷恩博告诉《新丽人》说，她现在在各种各样的客户脸上文雀斑，有夏天被晒出斑点想在日照不足的时候还保留这些晒斑的客户，也有脸上没雀斑却一直梦想拥有自己的雀斑的客户。

这位美容文身技师说："雀斑'刚做好'的时候，看上去肿得像被蜜蜂蜇过，但是几个小时后，肿胀就会消下去，你就能拥有你的可爱新雀斑了。再过一到两个月，雀斑的颜色就会变淡很多，看上去更自然。这些雀斑会随着时间流逝慢慢淡去，如果你想保留雀斑，可以随时去增强一下颜色。"

加布里埃尔·雷恩博说，她一般都觉得雀斑刺青"少即是多"，但是大多数客户都很喜欢刺青的效果，所以客户通常都要求文更多雀斑。然而，技师指出，有意文脸的人应该在做刺青之前先调查研究一番。近来要求文雀斑的人太多，无知的客户很容易被利用，所以雷恩博建议找那些敢于展示自己的刺青成果的技师。

雷恩博说："就算这个刺青是'半永久'的，也是存在风险的，比如技师可能针扎得太深，或者没有用合适的染料。" 绘英语

Here's to the Girls Who Don't Wear Makeup

文◎ anonymous

  Here's to the girls who don't wake up with perfect hair, who don't mind eating a Big Mac instead of salad, who don't wear 50 pounds of makeup, who'd rather spend the day in sweatpants than skinny jeans, who love the comfort of T-shirts, who stick to sneakers instead of heels, who don't always get their own way, who don't get everything they want, who don't need a guy to tell them that they are beautiful. Here's to all the girls who are just like me.

献给那些不化妆的女孩

文◎佚名

　　献给那些起床时头发蓬乱的女孩，那些吃巨无霸汉堡而不是沙拉的女孩，那些不化妆的女孩，那些穿宽松运动裤而不穿紧身牛仔裤的女孩，那些喜欢穿舒适 T 恤的女孩，那些坚持穿运动鞋而不穿高跟鞋的女孩，那些不任性的女孩，那些并不是想要什么就能得到什么的女孩，那些不需要男人告诉她有多漂亮的女孩。谨以此献给那些，像我一样平凡无奇的女孩。绘英语

You Can Set the Standards on Beauty by Yourself

文◎ anonymous

"If you had to choose, would you prefer a woman with a hot body or a beautiful face?" It's a classic question that every woman wants to ask their boyfriend.

I once read an article that said, nowadays, some women wouldn't let their boyfriends see their real face.

Part of the reason they behave this way is people impose stereotyped ideas about beauty on them. The other part of the reason is they are not confident enough about themselves.

So, instead of asking men to answer this question, women should bear in mind that the scope of beauty is getting broader and broader. Only when they really appreciate their own beauty, will they become more confident.

"I feel free, once I realized I was never going to fit the narrow mold that society wanted me to fit in," reads a quote from Ashley Graham, the first plus-size model to appear on the cover of *Vogue*.

We don't want to see similar beautiful faces on the street, looking like products from the same assembly line.

Don't label yourself a certain kind of woman. Be the woman that gets to decide who you are and how you should look. Being different is beautiful; being confident is beautiful; being real is beautiful.

无须别人告诉你什么才是美丽

文◎佚名

"如果你不得不做出选择，你会选择身材好还是颜值高的女人？"这是一个老生常谈的问题，每个女人都想这样问她们的男友。

我曾经读过的一篇文章称，现今一些女性不会让她们的男友看到自己的素颜。

她们之所以会这样做，部分原因是人们会将关于美丽的刻板印象强加在她们身上。而另一部分原因则是女性不够自信。

因此，女人们不应该叫男人回答这个问题，而是要在心里谨记，美丽的范围正变得越来越广。只有当女人真正懂得欣赏自己的美丽之后，她们才会变得更加自信。

时尚杂志《服饰与美容》第一个大码超模阿什利·格雷厄姆有一句名言："当我意识到我不会委屈自己缩进这个社会想让我适应的狭窄模具时，我就感觉到了自由。"

我们并不想在街上看到虽然很美，却像同一个流水线生产出来的产品一样的脸庞。

不要给自己贴上是某种女人的标签。你应该成为那种自己决定自己是谁、自己决定自己是什么样子的女人。与众不同就是美，充满自信就是美，真实不虚就是美！

How Can You Be the New It Girl

文◎ anonymous

I was reading an *Instyle* magazine article featuring Sharon Stone. You know, that *Basic Instinct* actress who happens to be a genius, with an IQ worthy of Mensa.

At 47, she still is a stunner. The sexy blonde woman who raises the temperatures of men is far from abimbo. As a kid, she would hide in her closet, reading, of all things, the encyclopedia.

Brainy girls usually end up as geeks in school. Or do they?

Is Sharon Stone a geek?

Now that would be hard to imagine. Apparently, the summer before her senior year, she blossomed into a glamour girl. She bought new boots, white jeans, changed her name, and went back to school as the new girl, from a geek to the beauty guys want to date.

Geek or prom queen? It is all in the way you present yourself.

Take the new term as a chance to reinvent yourself completely. Your studies need not be affected. You can still put in as much dedication to your school work as before your image change, but that does not mean you have to look like a geek to be smart.

Start off by switching from glasses to contact lenses. That alone makes a world of difference.

You might want to go all the way be changing your hair color. Go to a professional to have it done the first time around. With the help of an experienced stylist, get the ideal hair color and cut to suit your coloring and face shape.

If you like, you can even change the color of your eyes with colored contact lenses.

If you do not use make up, now is the time to begin. Start with the basics. Black mascara and a few lipsticks you can mix around to create different colors. Black mascara is dramatic. It darkens and lengthens your eye lashes, framing your eyes beautiful. As for the lipsticks, get at least 3 lipsticks. 1 red lipstick, 1 darker brown lipstick and 1 lighter pink lipstick. With these, you can mix the colors to get countless different shades of flattering lip colors. Experiment with these to create your new look. A day look and a night look.

Next comes the wardrobe revamp. Rather than get lots of cheap items, invest in a few key items you would wear every day. Get a pair of jeans that makes you look your very best, a gorgeous jacket and a pair of great looking boots. These 3 items can define your new look.

Now get a few tops you can wear each day. Blouses

are back, so a pretty blouse is a must. A few long sleeved t-shirts, well chosen are what you need next. Finally, a beautiful wrap would complete that look.

If you have the time, go for deportment classes. Better yet, go for modelling classes to learn to walk like a model on the catwalk.

With your new look, wardrobe and walk, you'll turn heads as the new girl in school.

如何成为一个崭新的酷女孩

文◎佚名　译◎Sherry Liu（雪莉·刘）

我从《风尚》杂志中读到一篇关于莎朗·斯通的文章。这位《本能》里的女主角现实生活中也是一位智商极高的女性。她的智商甚至已经可以达到门撒国际（高智商者的组织，成员的智商高于148）的标准。

而47岁的她现在仍然是一位绝世佳人。这位拥有性感金发、令男人神魂颠倒的女人并非人们传统概念里的轻浮无脑的女性。当她是个孩子的时候，她便会躲在自己的衣柜里，博览群书。

然而，聪明的女孩最终通常会成为学校里的怪人。可事实真的如此吗？

莎朗·斯通是一个怪胎吗？

现在看来，这个结论是不可理喻的。高中之前的那个夏天，

显然，莎朗已经成了一个魅力四射的女孩。她买了新鞋和白色牛仔裤，并且换了新的名字，以一个崭新的形象重新回到学校生活中。她从一个怪胎变成了一个帅小伙们都想要交往的尤物。

一个人是怪人还是舞会王后？这都在于你展现自己的方式。

我们应该抓住新的人生起点，重塑自我。但这并不意味着你的学习会受到影响。你仍然可以把尽可能多的时间和精力像形象改变以前那样投入学业中，然而这不需要你看起来像一个聪明的怪胎。

首先，摘下你的眼镜，戴上隐形眼镜。光这一点就会使你的世界大变模样。

其次，你会想尽办法去改变头发的颜色。那么你要第一时间到专业的美发店去做个新发型。在有经验的设计师的帮助下，不管是你的发色还是发型都会变得理想，而且很好地衬出你的肤色和脸形。

再次，如果你愿意，你甚至可以利用美瞳来改变你眼睛的颜色。

如果你没有化过妆，那么现在是时候开始了。请先从基础开始。你可以将黑色睫毛膏和一些唇膏混搭来形成不同的颜色搭配。黑色睫毛膏是极其神奇的，它会使你的眼睫毛变黑、延长，眼睛更加漂亮迷人。至于唇膏，你至少要有三支：一支红色的，一支暗棕色的，以及一支浅粉红色的。有了这些，你可以混合不同的色彩，形成颜色深浅不一的、迷人的性感双唇。通过这些尝试你便可以重塑自己的面貌。白天一个样子，晚上一个样子。

接下来是衣柜的改造。与其买许多廉价的衣服，还不如花钱买几件像样的每天都可以穿的衣服。买一条让你看起来最漂亮的牛仔裤，一件上档次的外套和一双好看的靴子。通过这三件衣服你便可以确定一个新的面貌。

现在买了几件像样的、你每天都可以穿的衣服，当然还需衬衫陪衬，因此一件漂亮的衬衫是必需的。另外，精心挑选的几件长袖 T 恤是你接下来所需要的。最后，一个漂亮的披肩将完成最后的造型。

如果你有时间，就要去上个仪态班。更好的方法是去模特班学习如何更好看地走路，就像在 T 台上走秀一样。

有了新面貌，新衣服，新走路姿势，那么你将会成为学校里一个崭新的女孩。

Learn to Love the Person in the Mirror

文◎ anonymous

Dear Teenage Girl,

　　You yearned for your thirteenth birthday. On that day, you could finally announce to the world that you are officially a teenager. What exactly is the draw of being a teenager? Maybe it's the idea of more independence and adventure. Maybe it's the hope of going on a first date and getting that first kiss. Despite all of these exciting prospects, you quickly realized that the reality of being a teenager doesn't quite match the dream you had of it.

　　You have never prepared yourself for the first time someone called you ugly—and actually meant it. You have never guessed that one day you would look in the mirror and hate what you saw. You have never expected that you could feel so alone and misunderstood. In all likelihood, the mirror has become your enemy and an ally to that voice inside your head that is always tearing you down. But here's the thing: You can and should learn to love the person staring back at you in the mirror because that person is beautiful and completely unique. It's not as difficult as it may seem.

　　Take control over that voice in your head. The thoughts are your own and you can change them for better or for worse. When you look in the mirror, force that voice to say something positive rather than something negative. You can see all your flaws staring you in the face because you know yourself better than anyone else. Practice looking at yourself the way others see you, and that voice will almost certainly find something good to say about you. In the same way you see everything that's good about other people, they see your virtues.

Believe people when they call you pretty. I understand how hard it is to listen when people call you pretty. I do. You automatically assume they are lying to try to make you feel better or to flatter you. Stop doing that. People tell you that you look pretty because you do. The fact that you think of yourself as ugly has no bearing on how other people perceive you. Learn to take compliments, especially from the people that know you and love you. They are sincere.

Understand the mean girl's motive. I know that there is that one girl, maybe several girls, in your life who takes every chance to make you feel bad about yourself. Perhaps she is subtle about it, making snide comments about something you're wearing or how you did your hair. Perhaps she talks about you behind your back to other girls and you overhear it. Whichever way she mounts her attacks, just know this: That girl struggles with the same feelings you do. Anyone who feels the need to constantly bash others cannot possibly have a good self-image. You might have much more in common with that mean girl than you think.

Most importantly, listen when people tell you that what's on the inside counts the most. You've heard people

say this over and over again. You are sick and tired of being told that having a good personality trumps having good looks. But I'm here to tell you that it is 100 percent true. As I've grown older, I've come to realize that I value kindness much more than "beauty". I think my friends are absolutely gorgeous, of course, but that's not the reason I like them at all. Who cares if someone looks fabulous if they act awfully? You should be striving to make that person in the mirror someone who will bring joy to people.

Learning to love the person you see in the mirror is a struggle that every teenage girl experiences. But if you know what is the most important in life, then that lesson is an easier one to learn. Understand that being considered pretty is not what life is about. If you make life about having good looks, you won't live a happy or satisfied life. Instead, be a true friend to the people who need it most and focus on all of the people in your life who care about you. They care about you because you are who you are, and they would hate it if you changed. When you look in the mirror, smile, because the person there is more than a beautiful face. Smile because the person there is a beautiful person.

Kendra Freeman

试着爱镜中的自己

文◎佚名

亲爱的青春期少女：

你渴望着你的十三岁生日。在那天，你终于可以向全世界宣布你是法律上规定的青少年了。究竟是什么吸引你做一个青少年呢？或许是可以更独立、可以去冒险的想法，或许是对第一次约会和接吻的期待。尽管存在所有这些令人兴奋的前景，你很快就

意识到成为一名青少年的现实与你之前的梦想并不匹配。

第一次有人说你丑——并且真心觉得你丑时——你根本没有做好准备。你从未想过有一天你会看着镜子，恨里面的那个人。你从未想过你会感觉如此孤独，不为人理解。十有八九，镜子已经变成了你的敌人和你脑海中总是在诋毁你的那个声音的同盟。但事情是这样的：你可以也应该学着爱镜子里看着你的那个人，因为她漂亮、独一无二。这件事并没有看起来那么难。

控制你脑海中那个声音。那些想法是你自己的，你可以把它们变好或者变坏。当你看着镜子时，努力让那个声音说些积极的事情，而不是消极的事情。当凝视自己的脸时，你能看到你所有的缺陷，因为你比任何人都了解自己。练习用别人看你的方式来看待自己，几乎可以肯定那个声音一定会找到一些好的事情来说你。你看到别人身上的所有优点，别人也同样可以看到你身上的优点。

当别人说你漂亮时，相信他们。我理解在别人说你漂亮时相信他们有多难，真的。你不自觉地认为他们在说谎，只是为了尽力让你感觉好一点儿或者奉承你。别再那样做了。人们告诉你你看起来很漂亮，是因为你真的很漂亮。你认为自己长得丑这件事跟别人如何看你没有关系。学着接受赞美，尤其是来自了解你、爱你的人的赞美。他们是真心的。

理解坏女孩的动机。我知道在你的生命中会有一个或者几个女孩抓住每一个机会让你感觉很糟糕。或许她工于心计，总是挖苦你穿的衣服或者做的发型。或许她在背后和其他女孩说

你的坏话被你无意中听到了。不管她如何攻击你,要知道,那个女孩和你一样,都在和那种感觉做斗争。任何一个需要不断诋毁别人的人都不可能有良好的个人形象。你与那个坏女孩之间的共同点可能比你认为的要多得多。

最重要的是,当人们告诉你内在最重要的时候,要听从他们的意见。你已无数次听过人们这样说。你厌倦了被人告诫拥有好的性格胜过拥有美貌。但是,在这里我要告诉你那种说法百分之百正确。现在我已经长大,我意识到相比美貌我更看重善良。当然,我认为我的朋友们绝对都很靓丽,但那根本不是我喜欢他们的原因。如果一个人的行为很恶劣的话,谁会在乎他的外表是否美丽呢?未来你应该致力于让镜中人成为一个给人们带来快乐的人。

学着爱你在镜子里看见的人对每一个青春期少女来说都非易事。但如果你懂得生命中最重要的是什么,那门课就会变得容易了。要知道,被人认为漂亮并不是人生的全部。如果你认为人生的意义在于拥有美貌,你将得不到幸福满足的生活。相反,做最需要你的人真正的朋友,关心生活中所有关心你的人。他们关心你是因为你是你,如果你变了,他们会感到遗憾。照镜子时微笑,因为那里面的人不仅拥有一张漂亮的脸蛋,更因为那里面的人是美丽的。

肯德拉·弗里曼 绘英语

艾米莉亚·克拉克备受欢迎，无疑是因为她在《权力的游戏》中扮演的卡丽熙·龙之母丹妮莉丝·坦格利安一角。总而言之，粉丝们已经习惯了看她金色顺滑的长发发髻，但是艾米莉亚表示很多粉丝都不知道她是戴的假发。

I Was Wearing a Wig, No One Could Be Perfect Like that

文◎ Emilia Clarke

"I feel bad when I meet people and they realize I'm Khaleesi, and they get disappointed because we look nothing alike. I'm like, 'Sorry, that ain't really me! It's a wig.' No human is that beautiful."

And, she truly is a Khaleesi for the people because she's struggled with confidence just like the rest of us:

"I really 'struggled with my confidence growing up.' I thought I was too fat. I thought I was ugly.

I called myself the Cabbage Patch Kid. If a boy talked to me, I'd be shocked.

But then there's a special moment that happens as a young adult when you start to find out who you are, what you like, how you take your coffee, the people who make you feel good and who you should be around.

You begin to see beyond what your face or body looks like."

Honestly, at the end of the day, "when you're happy, that's beauty."

我戴的是假发，
没有人能长那么完美

文◎艾米莉亚·克拉克

"我很难过，因为每次有人遇到我、认出我就是卡丽熙时，他们都会因为觉得我和卡丽熙相差太远而失望。我就会说，'抱歉我不是长那样！那是假发。'没有人能长那么美。"

"我真的'从小就不太自信'，以前我总觉得自己太胖了，也不漂亮。

我总叫自己圆白菜娃娃。如果一个男生跟我讲话，我都会觉得不可思议。

然后到了某一时刻，你会逐渐认识自己，发现自己喜欢什么、喝咖啡加不加糖和奶，知道自己和哪一类人在一起相处舒服。

你逐渐开始在意长相和体型之外的东西。"

真的，一天结束时，"你开心就是美的。"

Madison Beer（麦迪逊·比尔）是美国歌手，因 Justin Bieber 发掘进入乐坛，曾与 Cody Simpson 合作单曲 *Valentine*。

I Was Embarrassed about My Ear

文◎ anonymous

Madison Beer has always felt self—conscious about one thing in particular. "I have never been a big fan of my ears." She preferred to cover them up and was afraid to rock a hairstyle that showed them off. "So when the messy bun started trending I was envious. I thought about trying the hairstyle many times but always felt like people would be staring at my ears if I did. "Over time, the singer finally realized her fear was silly and came to love her least favorite body part. "These are my ears. and I am thankful." she confides. "Now I rock that hair style about six days of the week!" Way to go, girl!

我的耳朵
曾经让我很尴尬

文◎佚名

麦迪逊·比尔一直特别在意一件事。"我一点儿都不喜欢我的耳朵。"她习惯把耳朵遮起来，害怕露出耳朵的发型，"所以发髻流行的时候，我真嫉妒那些留发髻的女孩子。我多次想尝试那个发型，但总是担心别人会盯着我的耳朵看，也就不了了之了。"随着时光的流逝，这位歌手终于意识到自己的担心是多余的，她逐渐爱上了原来最嫌弃的身体部位。她坦言："我的耳朵就是这样子，我充满感激，现在我每周有6天在梳发髻！"这就对啦，女孩！绘英语

Let's Learn How to Keep Smile

文◎ anonymous

  We all have our own idea of what the perfect smile should look like, whether we show a mouthful of pearly whites or keep our lips closed and turned up at the corners just so. New research suggests that there really is a proper way to smile, and it has everything to do with facial expression.

  When we think of the perfect smile, we often envision a wide, beaming grin, with all of our teeth showing. However, Nathaniel Helwig and his colleagues at the University of Minnesota discovered that a genuine smile actually rests less on showing teeth and more on facial

balance and symmetry.

Researchers looked at 3D computer-animated facial models of more than 800 participants. The computer-animated facial models underwent a series of facial transformations, with researchers changing the mouth angle, amount of teeth shown, the extent of the smile, and how symmetrical the smile was. Participants were then asked to rate the models' smiles based on effectiveness, genuineness, pleasantness, and perceived emotional intent.

The results of the study found that the most successful smile—one that was rated most pleasant, genuine, and effective—had a perfect balance of teeth, an ideal mouth angle, and a smile length that extended to what was dubbed the "sweet spot."

想当社交达人？
先学会保持微笑吧

文◎佚名

我们都有自己的想法，一个完美的笑容应该是什么样子，不管是露出你的大白牙齿，还是嘴角抬起，双唇上扬。一项新的研

究表明，正确的微笑，这与面部表情有着密切的关系。

当我们想到完美的微笑时，我们往往会想到一个露出所有牙齿的微笑。然而，明尼苏达大学的纳撒尼尔·赫尔维希和他的同事发现，真正的笑容实际上并不是露出几颗牙，而是更加均衡和对称的面部表情。

研究人员着眼于800多位参与者的3D电脑动画面部模型。他们为这些模型做了一系列的面部转换，改变了这些模型嘴角的弧度、露出的牙齿的数量、微笑的程度以及微笑的对称度。然后参与者被要求基于有效性、真诚度、愉悦感以及所领会到的情感意图来为这些模型的微笑评分。

研究发现，最成功的微笑，也就是说，被认为是最愉快和最真诚的微笑，最有效的，它显示了牙齿非常匀称，嘴角弧度完美，微笑的时间也被认为是"最好的"。

告白的书

路渺且迢 / 有你就好

《那个神秘的宣愉小姐》
《余生,请对我好一点》
《冬夜有微光》
《绯色黎明》
《世界的另一个你》
《对方正在输入中》
《你是年少的欢喜》
《我不愿你一个人走过青春的荒芜,喜欢的少年是你》
《你是久爱、亦是心欢》
《从此晚安我自己》
《比心》
……